KU-253-033

The **AA** **POCKET**Guide

DUBLIN

Dublin: Regions and Best places to see

★ Best places to see 20–41

■ Featured sight

▮ Southside West 45–59

▮ Southside East 61–79

▮ Northside 81–99

Original text by Hilary Weston and Jackie Staddon

Updated by Anto Howard

© Automobile Association Developments Limited 2008
First published 2008

ISBN: 978-0-7495-5512-2

Published by AA Publishing, a trading name of Automobile Association Developments
Limited, whose registered office is Fanum House, Basing View, Basingstoke,
Hampshire RG21 4EA. Registered number 1878835.

Colour separation: Keenes, Andover
Printed and bound in Italy by Printer Trento S.r.l.

Front cover images: (t) AA/S L Day; (b) AA/S McBride
Back cover image: AA/S L Day

A03404
Maps in this title based on Ordnance Survey Ireland. Permit No. 8136
© Ordnance Survey Ireland and Government of Ireland
Transport map © Communicarta Ltd, UK

About this book

This book is divided into five sections.

Planning pages 6–19
Before You Go; Getting There; Getting
Around; Being There

Best places to see pages 20–41
The unmissable highlights of any visit
to Dublin

Exploring pages 42–99
The best places to visit in Dublin,
organized by area

Excursions pages 100–125
Places to visit out of town

Maps pages 129–144
All map references are to the atlas
section. For example, Temple Bar has
the reference ✚ 136 B2 – indicating the
page number and grid square in which it
is to be found

Contents

PLANNING

6 – 19

BEST PLACES TO SEE

20 – 41

EXPLORING

42 – 99

EXCURSIONS

100 – 125

INDEX & ACKNOWLEDGEMENTS

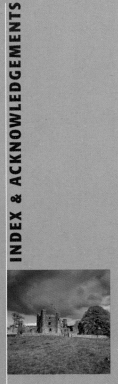

126 – 128

MAPS

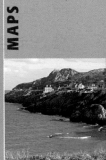

129 – 144

Planning

Before You Go	8–11
Getting There	12–13
Getting Around	14–15
Being There	16–19

Before You Go

WHEN TO GO

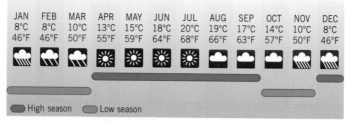

JAN	FEB	MAR	APR	MAY	JUN	JUL	AUG	SEP	OCT	NOV	DEC
8°C	8°C	10°C	13°C	15°C	18°C	20°C	19°C	17°C	14°C	10°C	8°C
46°F	46°F	50°F	55°F	59°F	64°F	68°F	66°F	63°F	57°F	50°F	46°F

High season   Low season

Temperatures are the **average daily maximum** for each month.

The best time to visit Dublin is between April and October, when the weather is at its best, although the city is very popular at any time of the year.

The peak tourist months are July and August; reserve accommodation early. Christmas and the New Year are also popular.

During November to March, the weather can be changeable. Most of the time it is cloudy, and frequently wet, dark and dreary. Autumn is generally fine, with a high percentage of crisp days and clear skies. Be prepared for rain at some time during your stay, no matter when you visit, but try to accept the rain as the Irish do – as a 'wet blessing'.

WHAT YOU NEED

● Required
○ Suggested
▲ Not required

Some countries require a passport to remain valid for a minimum period (usually at least six months) beyond the date of entry – contact their consulate or embassy or your travel agent for details.

	UK	Germany	USA	Netherlands	Spain
Passport (or National Identity Card where applicable)	●	●	●	●	▲
Visa (regulations can change – check before you travel)	▲	▲	▲	▲	▲
Onward or Return Ticket	▲	▲	▲	▲	▲
Health Inoculations (tetanus and polio)	▲	▲	▲	▲	▲
Health Documentation (▶ 9, Health Advice)	●	●	●	●	▲
Travel Insurance	○	○	○	○	○
Driving Licence (national)	●	●	●	●	●
Car Insurance Certificate	●	●	●	●	●
Car Registration Document	●	●	●	●	●

ADVANCE PLANNING
WEBSITES
www.visitdublin.com
www.dublin.ie
www.dublintourist.com
www.tourismireland.com

TOURIST OFFICES AT HOME
In the UK
Tourism Ireland
✉ 103 Wigmore Street, London, W1U 1QF
☎ 0800 039 7000

In the USA
Irish Tourist Board
✉ 345 Park Avenue, New York, NY 10154
☎ 212/418 0800

In Australia
Irish Tourist Board
✉ 5th Level, 36 Carrington Street, Sydney, NSW 2000
☎ 02 9299 6177

HEALTH ADVICE
Insurance
Nationals of EU and certain other countries can get medical treatment at reduced cost in Ireland with an EHIC (European Health Insurance Card, not required for UK nationals), although private medical insurance is still advised and is essential for all other visitors.

Dental services
EU nationals or nationals of countries with which Ireland has a reciprocal agreement can also get dental treatment within the Irish health service on production of an EHIC (not needed for UK nationals). Others should take out private medical insurance.

TIME DIFFERENCES

GMT	Ireland	Germany	USA (NY)	Netherlands	Spain
12 noon	12 noon	1PM	7AM	1PM	1PM

Ireland observes Greenwich Mean Time (GMT), but from late March, when clocks are put forward one hour, until late October, summertime (GMT +1) operates.

WHAT'S ON WHEN

January *New Year's Day Parade:* Marching bands from all over the world come together in Dublin for the parade.

February *International Film Festival:* The best Irish and international cinema is shown over a period of two weeks at this increasingly popular festival.

March *St Patrick's Day:* A popular date in Dublin's calendar, celebrated by a week of street entertainment, concerts, exhibitions and fireworks, building up to a huge parade on the day itself (17 March), usually starting near St Patrick's Cathedral.

May *Heineken Green Energy Music Festival:* Staged over the May bank holiday weekend, this major festival has featured top international stars since it began in the mid-1990s. There is normally an open-air concert in the grounds of Dublin Castle.

June *Bloomsday:* On 16 June each year, the day James Joyce set his novel *Ulysses*, Joycean fans celebrate the man and his works with tours, readings and seminars.

July *Dublin Jazz Festival:* A live, five-day schedule of music performed by artists from around the world. In Temple Bar and other locations.
Dublin Pride: The gay and lesbian scene is flourishing in Dublin, and this month-long festival is celebrated in a big way. It includes a free open-air show at the Civic Offices.

August *Dublin Horse Show:* The best show horses and show jumpers descend on the RDS grounds in the first week of August for Ireland's equine highlight of the year.
Liffey Swim: This has been a Dublin institution since 1924 – 400 or so people dive into the River Liffey in the centre of Dublin for a race through 2km (1.2 miles) of murky waters, while spectators line the bridges to watch.

NATIONAL HOLIDAYS

JAN	FEB	MAR	APR	MAY	JUN	JUL	AUG	SEP	OCT	NOV	DEC
1		3	2	1	1		1		1		2

1 January	New Year's Day
17 March	St Patrick's Day
March/April	Good Friday
March/April	Easter Monday
May (1st Mon)	May Holiday
June (1st Mon)	June Holiday
August (1st Mon)	August Holiday
October (last Mon)	All Soul's Day
25 December	Christmas Day
26 December	St Stephen's Day

Most shops, offices and museums close on these days. Good Friday is not a public holiday in the Republic, but many businesses observe it, so expect to find some offices, restaurants and pubs closed on this day.

September *Dublin Theatre Festival:* A two-week festival, among the most vibrant in Europe, attracting all the leading names from Dublin's drama scene. The many venues include the Abbey and the Gate theatres.

October *Dublin City Marathon:* On the last Monday in October thousands of enthusiastic runners turn out for the 42km (26-mile) run through the streets of Dublin. *Samhain:* An evening parade and fireworks for Dublin's Hallowe'en festival, based on the pagan festival of Samhain in celebration of the dead and the end of the Celtic summer.

December *Christmas National Hunt Festival:* A major four-day race meeting at Leopardstown racecourse.

Getting There

BY AIR

Regular flights operate from Britain, mainland Europe and North America. The national airline is Aer Lingus (☎ 844 4747; **www.**aerlingus.ie). Ryanair (☎ 844 4411; **www.**ryanair.com) offers low-cost flights. Dublin Airport is 11km (7 miles) from the centre, journey time 30 minutes by bus or 20 minutes by taxi.

● To get to Dublin city centre by car, take the M1 south. The journey takes between 20 minutes and an hour, depending on traffic.

● Taxis are always metered and a journey to the city centre should cost around €20.

● There are several bus options to reach Dublin city centre. **Airlink:** No 747 leaves every quarter hour for O'Connell Street, Busáras (the central bus terminal) and Parnell Square; No 748 also goes to Tara Street, Aston Quay and Heuston Station. Tickets are available at the CIE Information Desk in Arrivals. For information, contact Dublin Bus (☎ 01 873 4222; **www.**dublinbus.ie). **Aircoach** express: operates 5am–midnight, with departures every 15 minutes for city-centre stops including O'Connell Street, Grafton Street, Merrion Square North, Pembroke Road and St Stephen's Green; get tickets from the Tourist Information desk in Arrivals. Contact Aircoach (☎ 01 844 7118; **www.**aircoach.ie) for information. The cheapest way into the city is by **public bus** (Nos 16A, 41, 41A, 41B and 41C), but they are slower than Airlink and Aircoach services because they make many stops along the way; buses leave every 10–20 minutes for Eden Quay, near O'Connell Street.

BY SEA

● Ferries from the UK sail into the ports of Dublin, 5km (3 miles) east of the city, and Dun Laoghaire (pronounced 'Dunleary'), 14km (9 miles) south of the city.
● If travelling by **car,** simply follow city-centre signs.

- **Taxis** operate from both ports into the centre of Dublin, with a journey time of around 20 minutes.
- There's an inexpensive **DART** service (➤ 28) from Dun Laoghaire to Dublin, running half-hourly (sometimes more often) to Pearse, Tara Street and Connolly stations in the city centre. The journey takes 25 minutes.
- **Public buses** run regularly: Nos 7, 7A, 46A or 46X from Dun Laoghaire DART Station; Nos 53 or 53A from Dublin Port. Dublin Bus operates a shuttle service to Busáras (the central bus station) every half-hour 7am–11.10pm. The journey takes around 30 minutes.

BY TRAIN

- Dublin has two mainline stations: Connolly serves the north, Heuston serves the south and west of Ireland. Buses and taxis are available at both stations. For rail information, contact Irish Rail/Iarnród Éireann (☎ 01 836 6222; **www.**irishrail.ie).

DRIVING

Drive on the left.

Speed limit on motorways **112kph/ 70mph;** dual carriageways: **96kph/60mph.** Speed limit on country roads: **96kph/60mph.** Speed limit on urban roads: **48kph/30mph** (or as signposted).

Seatbelts must be worn in front seats at all times and in rear seats where fitted.

Random breath-testing takes places. Never drive under the influence of alcohol.

Lead replacement petrol (LRP) and unleaded petrol are widely available. Many fuel stations in and around Dublin stay open 24 hours, while those in the villages and more rural areas stay open until 8 or 9pm, and open after Mass on Sundays.

If you break down driving your own car and are a member of an AIT-affiliated motoring club, you can call the Automobile Association's rescue service (☎ 1800 667788). If the car is rented follow the instructions given in the documentation; most of the international rental firms provide a rescue service.

Getting Around

PUBLIC TRANSPORT

Internal flights Flights from Dublin to other airports in Ireland are operated by Aer Lingus (► 12) and Aer Arann (☎ 814 1058; **www**.aerarann.ie).

Trains Ireland has a limited network run by Iarnród Éireann (☎ 703 2358; **www**.irishrail.ie), which serves major towns and cities. Dublin has two main stations; trains from the north arrive at Connolly Station and trains from the south and west arrive at Heuston Station.

Long-distance buses Bus Éireann (☎ 836 6111; **www**.buseireann.ie) operates a network of express bus routes out of Dublin serving most of the country (some run during summer only).

Urban transport The city's extensive bus service is run by Dublin Bus (59 Upper O'Connell Street; ☎ 872 0000; **www**.dublinbus.ie). As there are so many different buses that run across the city, Dublin Bus provides free individual timetables for each route. The Rapid Transit system (DART) runs along the coast from Malahide in the north to Greystones in the south (☎ 836 6222; **www**.irishrail.ie/dart). The LUAS light railway operates from the centre out to the suburbs. A range of fare-saving combined travel passes is available.

TAXIS

Taxi stands are outside hotels, train and bus stations, and at major locations such as St Stephen's Green, Dame Street, O'Connell Street and Dawson Street. Taxis can be hailed on the street but late at night they can be in short supply so you might have to wait in line.

Radio Cabs ☎ 677 2222
City Cabs ☎ 872 7272

CAR RENTAL

Car rental in Dublin is expensive. All of the main international car rental companies are represented, however, a car from a local company is likely to be cheaper, but may not allow different pick-up/drop-off points. For July and August it is best to make reservations well ahead.

CONCESSIONS

Students Students under 18 are entitled to reduced entrance in some museums and galleries. Be sure to carry some form of identification. Holders of an International Student Identity Card can buy a Travelsave Stamp entitling them to travel discounts, including a 50 per cent reduction on Bus Éireann, Iarnród Éireann and Irish Ferries (between Britain and Ireland). Contact your local student travel agency for further details. The Travelsave Stamp can be purchased from USIT (19 Aston Quay, Dublin 2; **www**.usit.ie; ☎ 602 1777).

Senior citizens Senior citizens (over 60) are entitled to discounts on transport and most admission fees, on proof of age.

Being There

TOURIST OFFICES
● Fáilte Ireland, Baggot Street Bridge, Baggot Street, Dublin 2
☎ 602 4000; **www.**failteireland.ie

● Dublin Tourism, St Andrew's Church, Suffolk Street, Dublin 2
☎ 605 7700; **www.**visitdublin.com

Walk-in centres
14 Upper O'Connell Street, Dublin Airport, Dun Laoghaire ferry terminal, The Square, Tallaght (southern suburbs).

East Coast & Midlands Tourism
Market House, Market Square, Mullingar, Co Westmeath ☎ 044 48650; **www.**eastcoastmidlands.ie

EMBASSIES AND CONSULATES
UK ☎ 205 3700
Germany ☎ 269 3011
USA ☎ 668 8777
Netherlands ☎ 269 3444
Spain ☎ 269 1640

TELEPHONES
Public telephone boxes are either blue and cream or the newer glass-booth style, and take coins or phone cards (sold at post offices and newsagents). The Dublin code is 01; dial 10 for national operator assistance and 114 for the international operator. All numbers preceded with 1800 are toll-free.

OPENING HOURS

- Shops
- Offices
- Banks
- Post offices
- Museums/monuments
- Pharmacies

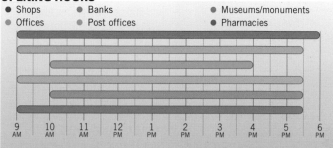

| 9 AM | 10 AM | 11 AM | 12 PM | 1 PM | 2 PM | 3 PM | 4 PM | 5 PM | 6 PM |

In addition to times shown above, some shops open on Sunday. Late-night shopping is on Thursday, with many places open until 8pm. Most banks close on Saturdays; some remain open till 5pm on Thursdays.

City-centre post offices open on Saturday mornings. Pharmacies display a list of pharmacies that open at night and on Sundays.

Museum hours vary according to the season, so always check ahead.

EMERGENCY TELEPHONE NUMBERS
Police 999
Fire 999
Ambulance 999
Coastal Rescue 999

INTERNATIONAL DIALLING CODES
From Ireland to:

UK: 00 44
USA: 00 1
Germany: 00 49
Netherlands: 00 31
Spain: 00 34
Australia: 00 61

POSTAL SERVICES
The main post office, in O'Connell Street, opens Mon–Sat 8–8; hours for other post offices are generally Mon–Fri 9–5.30, Sat 9–1. Post-boxes are green; stamps are sold at post offices, some newsagents or are available from machines.

ELECTRICITY
The power supply is 240 volts AC. Sockets are generally the UK type, with three square pins. Parts of the Republic also have two round pins (Continental type). Overseas visitors should bring a voltage transformer and plug adaptor.

come in €5, 10, 20, 50, 100, 200 and 500 denominations (the last two are rarely seen). The notes and one side of the coins are the same throughout the European single currency zone, but each country has a different design on one face of each of the coins.

HEALTH AND SAFETY

Sun advice The sunniest months are June and July with on average 5–6.5 hours of sun a day, though July and August are the hottest. During these months you should take precautions – cover up, use a good sunscreen and drink plenty of water.

Drugs Prescription and non-prescription drugs and medicines are available from pharmacies. When closed, most pharmacies display details of the nearest one that is open. In an emergency, contact the nearest hospital.

CURRENCY

The euro (€) is the official currency of the Republic of Ireland, which is divided into 100 cents. Coins come in denominations of 1, 2, 5, 10, 20 and 50 cents, €1 and 2, and notes

TIPS/GRATUITIES

Yes ✓   No ✗

Restaurants (if service not included)	✓	10%
Cafés/bars (if service not included)	✓	10%
Taxis	✓	10%
Porters	✓	€1
Tour guides	✓	€2
Cloakroom attendants	✓	€1
Hairdressers	✓	€2
Theatre usherettes	✗	
Toilets	✗	

Safe water Tap water in Ireland is perfectly safe to drink. However, if you prefer to drink bottled water you will find it widely available, though it is often expensive, particularly in restaurants.

PERSONAL SAFETY

Until recently, street crime was rare in Dublin, but petty crime is on the increase.
● Keep valuables in your hotel safe.
● Pickpockets and bag snatching are prevalent.
● Watch handbags and wallets in public places.
● Avoid Phoenix Park and poorly lit alleys and side-streets after dark.
● Keep cars well secured and avoid leaving property in view.

The national police, called the Garda Síochána (pronounced shee-kaw-nah), wear blue uniforms and, in bad weather, yellow raincoats.
Police assistance:
☎ 999 from any call box

PHOTOGRAPHY

Best times to photograph: early morning and late evening. Irish light can be dull so you may need faster film eg 200 or 400 ASA.
Where to buy film: most film and camera batteries are readily available in many shops and pharmacies.

CLOTHING SIZES

France	UK and Ireland	Rest of Europe	USA	
46	36	46	36	
48	38	48	38	
50	40	50	40	
52	42	52	42	
54	44	54	44	**Suits**
56	46	56	46	
41	7	41	8	
42	7.5	42	8.5	
43	8.5	43	9.5	
44	9.5	44	10.5	
45	10.5	45	11.5	**Shoes**
46	11	46	12	
37	14.5	37	14.5	
38	15	38	15	
39/40	15.5	39/40	15.5	
41	16	41	16	
42	16.5	42	16.5	**Shirts**
43	17	43	17	
36	8	34	6	
38	10	36	8	
40	12	38	10	
42	14	40	12	
44	16	42	14	**Dresses**
46	18	44	16	
38	4.5	38	6	
38	5	38	6.5	
39	5.5	39	7	
39	6	39	7.5	
40	6.5	40	8	**Shoes**
41	7	41	8.5	

Best places to see

Christ Church Cathedral   22–23

Dublin Castle and Chester
    Beatty Library   24–25

General Post Office   26–27

Guinness Storehouse   28–29

James Joyce Centre   30–31

Kilmainham Gaol   32–33

National Gallery   34–35

National Museum   36–37

St Patrick's Cathedral   38–39

Trinity College and the
    Book of Kells   40–41

1 Christ Church Cathedral

www.cccdub.ie

Dublin's oldest stone building and stronghold of the Protestant faith in Ireland was saved from ruin by extensive Victorian restoration.

Built on the site of the Norse king Sitric Silkenbeard's wooden church of 1038, this Romanesque and early Gothic church was commissioned in 1172 by Richard de Clare, the Anglo-Norman conqueror of Dublin – better known as Strongbow – for Archbishop Laurence O'Toole. The archbishop later became St Laurence, patron of Dublin, whose heart remains in the cathedral in a 13th-century metal casket.

After Henry VIII broke with Rome, Robert Castle, the last prior of the Augustinian priory of Holy Trinity, became the first dean of Christ Church in 1541. In 1562 the nave roof vaulting collapsed, crushing Strongbow's tomb and leaving the cathedral in ruins. Temporary measures to shore up the damage remained in place until the 1870s, and the roof, to the present day, still leans out by 46cm (18in). During the 16th and 17th centuries Christ Church's crypt was used as a market, a meeting place and even a pub. Heavy restoration at the expense of Henry Roe, a local whiskey distiller, was

undertaken by architect George Edmund Street in the 1870s. Although little remains of the original Norman structure – only the south transept and the crypt – the cathedral was saved from complete decay. Further work took place in the 1980s and 1990s, including the restoration of the 12th-century crypt. This contains an intriguing range of relics and objects, including the old wooden punishment stocks. The exhibition 'Treasures of Christ Church' reflects 1,000 years of history, architecture and worship in Ireland.

✚ 135 C8 ✉ Christchurch Place ☎ 677 8099 🕔 Jun–Aug daily 9–6; Sep–May daily 9.45–5 ✋ Moderate 🚆 Tara Street 🚌 Cross-city buses ↔ Dvblinia (➤ 48)

2 Dublin Castle and Chester Beatty Library

www.dublincastle.ie
www.cbl.ie

Situated on a strategic ridge, the castle is at the heart of historic Dublin. Visit the gallery and library in the gardens.

Dublin Castle was the headquarters of British rule for over 700 years. Little remains of the original structure, except for the modified Record Tower (containing the Garda Museum), and the mixture of architectural styles and government offices mask the fact that this was originally a Viking fortress. The castle stands on the site of the black pool or *dubh linn* from which the city took its name.

Following a fire in 1684, more stately accommodation was built to replace the medieval interior, including the lavish Throne Room and the Ballroom or St Patrick's Hall, where the ceiling fresco is considered the most important painted ceiling in Ireland. The neo-Gothic Chapel Royal was added in 1807 and displays carved stone likenesses of a hundred British dignitaries. The Undercroft was revealed after excavations in 1990 and can be visited on a tour. Here you will see part of the original Viking fortress and, in the base of the Norman Powder Tower, some of the Viking defensive bank.

The **Chester Beatty Library** is housed in the Clock Tower Building and has a rich collection of artistic treasures from the great cultures and religions of the world. The manuscripts, prints, icons, books and other objects were bequeathed to the nation in 1956 by Sir Alfred Chester Beatty (1875–1968). This successful American mining magnate became one of the few people to have been made an honorary citizen of Ireland.

Dublin Castle

✚ 136 C1 ✉ Castle Street ☎ 677 7129 ◷ Mon–Fri 10–5, Sat–Sun 2–5. Closed during state business ✋ Moderate 🍴 Castle Vaults Bistro (€–€€) 🚇 Tara Street 🚌 Cross-city buses

Chester Beatty Library

✚ 136 C1 ✉ Dublin Castle ☎ 407 0750 ◷ Mon–Fri 10–5, Sat 11–5, Sun 1–5. Closed Mon, Oct–Apr ✋ Free 🍴 Silk Road Café (€) 🚇 Tara Street 🚌 Cross-city buses

3 General Post Office

A significant building in the history of modern Ireland, the GPO was the main stronghold of the Irish Volunteers during the Easter Rising of 1916.

The imposing Palladian-style General Post Office in O'Connell Street was built in 1818, and while it is not one of Dublin's finest Georgian buildings, it is important in the history of Irish independence. It was from the steps of this building that Pádraic Pearse (1879–1916), leader of Irish nationalism, proclaimed Ireland a republic and no longer subject to British rule. He and his fellow volunteers resisted the British in a siege that lasted a week. Heavy bombardment forced the rebels out and the building was left severely ruined. The leaders of the uprising

were rounded up and 16 rebels were executed at Kilmainham Gaol (➤ 32–33), but the struggle against British rule continued and the siege at the Post Office highlights those years of struggle. The Irish Free State was finally formed five years later, in 1921.

The building, headquarters of An Post, the Irish Postal Service, re-opened in 1929. Despite heavy restoration, bullet holes can still be seen on the exterior walls. The building is a cross between a memorial to those who died and an everyday busy post office. Take a look inside at the remarkable bronze statue of the *Death of Cuchulainn* (by Oliver Sheppard, 1935), which depicts the demise of the legendary Irish hero Cuchulainn, and is dedicated to Pearse and the others who died in the Easter Rising. Note also the series of paintings depicting the Rising, in the manner of Communist propaganda posters. The building remains the focus of official parades and a salute is given here at Dublin's annual St Patrick's Day parade.

✚ 136 A2 ✉ O'Connell Street ☎ 872 8888 🕐 Mon–Sat 8–8, Sun 10.30–6 ✋ Free 🚊 Tara Street 🚌 Cross-city buses

4 Guinness Storehouse

www.guinness.com

Every visitor to Dublin should sample at least one pint of the 'black stuff'. The Storehouse is the ideal place to do this and learn about its production at the same time.

Guinness is synonymous with Dublin, an institution, a dominant employer in the city for over two centuries and now a household name throughout the world. When Arthur Guinness decided to experiment with the English dark porter ale in 1759, little did he know that 200 years later his surname would be revered the world over. Indeed, the largest producer of Guinness is now Nigeria.

The Storehouse, opened in 2000 on the site of the original St James's Gate brewery, pays homage to the memory of that early discovery. The stunning glass central atrium, an innovative structure built into the listed building, is in the shape of a giant pint glass. The froth at the top of the pint is the Gravity Bar where you can sup your free pint at the end of your self-guided tour while enjoying panoramic views over the city. As you make your way up the pint glass you will go through the various production processes. The heady aroma of roasting hops pervade the air and you can touch and smell the individual ingredients. The water used in the production of Guinness is traditionally believed to come from the River Liffey; in fact it comes from the nearby Grand Canal. Further displays, all well labelled and some interactive, include machinery and transport vehicles. Check

out the excellent advertising section, including
examples of posters depicting the memorable
toucan and the famous 1929 advert proclaiming
'Guinness is Good for You'.

✚ 135 D5 ✉ St James's Gate ☎ 408 4800, info line 453
8364 🕒 Daily 9.30–5 (9.30–8, Jul–Aug) ✋ Expensive
🍴 Gravity Bar, Source Bar, Brewery Bar and restaurant
(€–€€) 🚆 51B, 78A, 123 🚌 LUAS ❓ Shop selling
Guinness memorabilia

5 James Joyce Centre

www.jamesjoyce.ie

The centre is dedicated to fostering and promoting awareness of James Joyce's significant contribution to modern literature. Here you will find all manner of Joycean memorabilia.

i have a special knack of putting the noose once in he can't get out.

TERENCE O'RYAN HEARD him and straightway brought him a crystal cup full of the foaming ebon ale

James Joyce (1882–1941) spent most of his adult life in Europe, but it was his childhood in Dublin that provided him with the setting and characters for his novels *Ulysses*, *Finnegans Wake* and *Dubliners*. Joyce did not live in this particular house but in the vicinity, which was at the time a run-down area with most houses needing repair. In 1982 Senator David Norris restored the 18th-century town house to its original glory and converted it into a centre of Joycean study. Among the most interesting exhibits is a fascinating set of biographies of some 50 characters from the most famous of Joyce's works, *Ulysses*, written between 1914 and 1921.

The centre organizes walking tours so you can trace the footsteps of the novel's hero, Leopold Bloom, as he walked around the city on 16 June, 1904. During 2004, the centenary celebrations of

this event included special Bloomsday festivities throughout the city and around the world. Rejoyce 2004 also marked several months of activities and events based around the great master of the novel.

The James Joyce Centre also shows short films on Joyce and his Dublin, as well as recordings of him reading his own novels. A highlight of a visit is the current connection with members of Joyce's family and his nephew, Ken Monaghan, shows visitors around the house. Look out for the murals around the courtyard depicting the 18 chapters of *Ulysses*, painted by Paul Joyce, great-nephew of James Joyce. You can also see the original door of No 7 Eccles Street, the fictional home of Leopold Bloom.

✚ 133 F5 ✉ 35 North Great George's Street ☎ 878 8547 ⏱ Mon–Fri 9.30–12.30, 1.30–3.30 ✋ Moderate; tours of Joycean Dublin expensive 🚌 Cross-city buses ❓ Bookshop

6 Kilmainham Gaol

The gaol (jail) provides a moving insight into the grim reality of incarceration in Dublin's notorious prison. It remains a symbol of Ireland's fight for independence.

Inspired by the Bastille in Paris, Kilmainham Gaol was built in 1787, and remained a prison until 1924. It has held some of the most famous rebels in Ireland's history, including those from the rebellions of 1798, 1803, 1848, 1867, 1883 and, most famously, the 1916 Easter Rising. Visits are by guided tour only and start with a video presentation to set the grisly scene. The tour, which takes about 90 minutes, places the historical facts in context, emphasizing that this was a prison for civil as well as political prisoners. Petty criminals were also incarcerated here, including many victims of the Great Famine of 1845–49, when stealing was rife. Up to 7,000 inmates, both men and women, were crammed into the dank and dark cells.

The prison closed in 1910 and was converted into barracks to house troops during World War I, but it was re-opened to receive the insurgents of the 1916 Easter Rising. The public execution of 16 of the rebels that took place here included Joseph Plunkett, who married Grace Gifford just 10 minutes before his execution. The last prisoner to be held here, in 1924, was Eámon de Valera, who went on to become president of Ireland. The abandoned gaol fell into decay, but because of its exceptional historical interest was restored by volunteer groups in the 1960s.

Among the areas included on the tour are the east- and west-wing cell blocks, the chapel, the exercise yard where the rebels were executed and the museum with its grim artefacts and Irish memorabilia.

✚ 134 D1 ✉ Inchicore Road, Kilmainham ☎ 453 5984
🕒 Apr–Sep daily 9.30–5; Oct–Mar Mon–Sat 9.30–4, Sun and public hols 10–5. Last tour 1 hour before closing
✋ Moderate 🍴 Tea room (€) 🚌 51B, 68, 69, 78A, 79; tram: LUAS ❓ Guided tours only – advisable to book

7 National Gallery

www.nationalgallery.ie

Home to one of Europe's premier collections of Old Masters, the National Gallery also displays home-grown talent, in particular the works of the Yeats family.

The gallery opened its doors to the public in 1864, in a building designed by Francis Fowke, the architect of the Victoria & Albert Museum in London. Beginning with just 125 paintings, the gallery's prime task was to inspire Irish artists of the day. The collection now has over 2,500 paintings and some 10,000 works in different media, including drawings, prints and sculptures.

The building consists of four wings: the original Dargan Wing, the Milltown Wing, the Beit Wing and the Millennium Wing, the latter housing a study centre of Irish work – complete with a Jack B Yeats archive – and temporary exhibition galleries.

The collections are vast and can be confusing, so pick up a floor plan. You may want to single out your own personal favourites rather than wander round each gallery. In the Millennium Wing is a multimedia gallery with computer touch screens where you can find out background information on paintings in the collection. Every major European school of painting is represented here. If it's Old Masters you're after, look out for works by Fra Angelico, Titian, Caravaggio, Rembrandt and Canova. Lovers of Impressionism can view works by Monet, Degas, Pissarro, Sisley and others. British artists such as Reynolds and Turner are also represented, as are modern painters up to Picasso.

Among the works of Jack B Yeats in the Yeats Museum are several Dublin cityscapes.

➕ 136 D4 ✉ Merrion Square West and Clare Street
☎ 661 5133 🕐 Mon–Sat 9.30–5.30, Thu 9.30–8.30, Sun
12–5.30 ✋ Free; expensive for special exhibitions
🍴 Restaurant and café (€–€€) 🚉 Pearse 🚌 Cross-city
buses ❓ Guided tours Sat 3pm, Sun 2, 3 and 4pm

8 National Museum

www.museum.ie

Ireland's rich heritage is brought to life in this superb building, one of Dublin's foremost attractions, with some of the best gold artefacts on display in Europe.

The collections are exhibited in a magnificent building of 1877. The splendid domed rotunda, which forms the entrance hall, has columns of Irish marble and a mosaic floor depicting the signs of the zodiac. This is the national repository for more than 2 million artefacts dating from 7000BC to the late medieval period.

Beginning with the prehistoric period, you will

find displays of tools and weaponry from the Stone and Bronze ages. Check out the 13m (42ft) Lurgan longboat. Dating from around 2500BC, it is Ireland's earliest surviving boat, hewn out of an oak tree. Other artefacts are in excellent condition, having been preserved in Ireland's peat bogs. The stunning Bronze Age gold jewellery of the 'Ór – Ireland's Gold' exhibition is unmatched in Europe

and the styles, surprisingly sophisticated, are still copied today. In the Treasury you can see several 8th-century gems including the Ardagh Chalice, a beautiful, gilded, twin-handled cup, and the stunning Tara brooch, intricately decorated with birds and animals. Look out for the gilt-bronze 12th-century Cross of Cong, with its silver wire, crystals and enamelled studs. On the same floor, the Road to Independence exhibition is a vivid portrayal of Ireland's turbulent political history from 1900 to the signing of the Anglo-Irish treaty of 1921.

Upstairs are the Viking Age Ireland and Medieval Ireland 1150–1550 collections, perhaps a little more down to earth after the magnificence of the earlier displays. The Clothes from Bogs in Ireland exhibition gathers together all the historic clothing found incredibly well preserved in Irish wetlands and bogs.

✚ 136 D3 ✉ Kildare Street ☎ 677 7444 🕐 Tue–Sat 10–5, Sun 2–5 ♿ Free 🍽 Café (€) 🚆 Pearse 🚌 Cross-city buses ❓ Guided tours from main entrance at regular intervals

St Patrick's Cathedral

www.stpatrickscathedral.ie

St Patrick's is Dublin's second great cathedral and the largest church in Ireland. It is a paradox that in a predominately Catholic city and country there should be two Protestant cathedrals.

Legend has it that St Patrick passed through Dublin on his travels in Ireland in the 5th century. A small wooden church was built on the spot where he converted several pagans to Christianity. On this same site the Anglo-Norman first bishop of Dublin, John Comyn, constructed a stone church, which was upgraded to cathedral status in 1219. It was built in the English Gothic style and finally completed in 1284. By the 19th century it was in a very poor state and lay almost derelict among slum housing. Much of the cathedral was rebuilt and restored between 1860 and 1900, paid for mainly by the Guinness family.

Just inside the building is the grave of one of the cathedral's most famous sons. The author and reformist Jonathan Swift

was dean here from 1713 to 1745 and he tried hard to preserve the building, but to no avail. The death mask, pulpit, chair and writing table of the great man are among memorabilia on display. Other highlights include the largest organ in the country, and you can also hear the largest peal of bells in Ireland. A particularly interesting memorial is the

one to the celebrated blind harpist Turlough O'Carolan (1670–1730). The exhibition 'Living Stones' celebrates the cathedral's role in city life and its place in the history of Dublin. It is important to remember that St Patrick's is not a museum but very much an active church and an integral part of city life.

✚ 135 D8 ✉ Patrick's Street ☎ 453 9472 🕓 Mar–Oct Mon–Sat 9–5.15, Sun 9–10.30, 12.30–2.30, 4.30–6; Nov–Feb Mon–Sat 9–5, Sun 10–11, 12.45–3 ✋ Moderate 🚌 Cross-city buses

10 Trinity College and the Book of Kells

www.tcd.ie

The oldest university in Ireland houses the Book of Kells, arguably one of the most

beautifully illuminated manuscripts in the world.

Trinity College is a peaceful oasis amid the hustle and bustle of modern Dublin.

The main entrance on College Green is next to one of the busiest roads in Dublin, but once inside you enter a different world. Parliament Square, with its 19th-century campanile and elegant 18th-century Dining Hall and Chapel, leads on to Fellows' Square, where old and new buildings blend sympathetically. The Old Library (1732), designed by Thomas Burgh, stands to the west; to the east is Benjamin Woodward's 19th-century carved Museum building; to the south Paul Koralek's New Library (1978).

Most visitors head straight for the Old Library to see the magnificent Book of Kells and other ancient illuminated manuscripts, housed in the darkened Treasury on the ground floor. Written on vellum around AD800, the Book of Kells is a superbly illustrated transcription of the Gospels. The exhibition 'Turning Darkness into Light' explains the

context of the book and how the monastic scribes produced such a sublime work of art, highly imaginative, with figures of humans and animals, and intricate Celtic patterns. It was discovered in the town of Kells in Co Meath, but is thought to have been created by four Irish monks on Iona, off the coast of Scotland. Apparently they fled from the Vikings to Ireland and finished the book in Kells. Two volumes can usually be seen, one opened to display the decorative work and one showing script. Other ornate manuscripts are on show.

The Long Room, upstairs from the Treasury, is nearly 65m (213ft) in length and houses around 200,000 books. The 15th-century harp on display here, believed to be the oldest in Ireland, is the harp that appears on Irish coins.

✚ 136 C3 ✉ College Street ☎ College: 608 2320; library: 608 2308 ⊕ College campus daily. Old Library and Book of Kells: May–Sep Mon–Sat 9.30–5, Sun 9.30–4.30; Oct–Apr noon–4.30 ✋ Campus free; Old Library and Book of Kells expensive 🚇 Tara Street 🚌 Cross-city buses ❓ College tours May–Sep. Douglas Hyde Gallery for temporary art exhibitions all year

Exploring

Southside West   45–59

Southside East   61–79

Northside   81–99

Dublin is a small city and very easy to explore. Walking is the best option, although there is an excellent bus service. The River Liffey provides a prominent landmark when navigating the city and most attractions are on the south side, including Temple Bar, Grafton Street, Trinity College and the Georgian district, with its renowned national museums and galleries. North of the river has always been considered the poor relation, but with restoration projects being carried out at Smithfield Village, O'Connell Street/Henry Street and the docks, it's taking on a smarter image. The renovation of Dublin is ongoing, with parts of the city seemingly forever under scaffolding. After dark, serious partygoers head for Temple Bar and its pubs and bars; it also has a wide selection of restaurants. For those who prefer a quieter evening, there are plenty of sophisticated restaurants, trendy bars and low-key pubs.

Southside West

This part of Dublin is one of the most historic and fascinating areas in the city, the place where the earliest Celtic settlers set up home, where the Vikings created their city more than 1,000 years ago and where, according to legend, St Patrick embarked on his mission to convert the Irish to Christianity. Here you will find some of the finest historic buildings, including the two medieval cathedrals (Christ Church and St Patrick's), Dublin Castle, the ceremonial heart of the modern Republic of Ireland, and the sombre and sobering Kilmainham Gaol.

Here too is one of the most vibrant areas of the city, the warren of narrow cobbled streets known as Temple Bar. Once a derelict, down-at-heel docklands area it's now home to trendy shops and galleries, pubs and restaurants, music venues and nightclubs – buzzing with activity at any time of the day or night. Beyond Temple Bar, most of the southwest part of the city is neither picturesque nor happening, but it draws visitors by the thousand because it contains one of the most famous institutions in Dublin – the Guinness Brewery and its interpretative centre, the Guinness Storehouse.

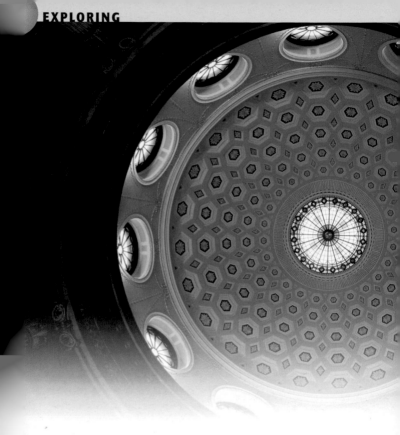

CHRIST CHURCH CATHEDRAL
See pages 22–23.

CITY HALL
This imposing building, with its striking Corinthian portico, was originally designed by Thomas Cooley between 1769 and 1779 to house the Royal Exchange, and became the headquarters of the Dublin Corporation in 1852. In 2000 the interior of the building was restored to its former Georgian magnificence. It's worth going inside just to admire its superb rotunda, stunningly lit by the huge windows. In the vaulted basement the multimedia exhibition 'The

Story of the Capital' tells the story of Dublin from its beginnings to the present day, with special attention to the development of civic government. There are displays of civic regalia, including the Great City Sword and the Great Mace. You can trace the history of Dublin through invasion, rebellion, civil war and plague, and the impact of the Viking, Norman, French-Huguenot and British rule on the city.

www.dublincity.ie/your_council/city_hall

✚ 136 C1 ✉ Cork Hill, Dame Street ☎ 672 2204 🕐 Mon–Sat 10–5.15, Sun and public hols 2–5 ♿ Moderate 🚌 Cross-city buses ↔ Dublin Castle (➤ 24–25)

DRIMNAGH CASTLE

You need to search for this one as it's hidden behind school buildings on the western outskirts of Dublin. But it's worth the effort as this is an outstanding example of an old feudal stronghold. Until 1954 it was one of the oldest continually inhabited castles in Ireland. The only Irish castle to have a full moat, it is set in a wonderfully restored 17th-century garden. From the 1950s the castle was in a bad state of repair and was not restored until the 1980s, when traditional craft skills were used to return it to its former glory.

✚ 134 F1 (off map) ✉ Long Mile Road, Drimnagh ☎ 450 2530 🕐 Wed 12–5, Sun 2–5 or by appointment ♿ Moderate 🍴 Tea room (€) 🚊 Drimnagh LUAS 🚌 18, 56, 77, 77A 🛍 Shop

DUBLIN CASTLE AND CHESTER BEATTY LIBRARY

See pages 24–25.

DVBLINIA

This award-winning exhibition reproduces the sights and sounds of medieval Dublin. Housed in the former Synod Hall, it is joined to Christ Church Cathedral by a bridge. Note that the bridge is only one way – into the cathedral – so visit Dvblinia first. Experience medieval life first hand through reconstructions of streets and houses. Major events in Dublin's history are re-created, including the Black Death and early rebellion. There are also artefacts removed from the excavation of nearby Wood Quay, which revealed Norse and Viking items such as pottery, coins and swords. From the top of St Michael's Tower there are great views of the city.
www.dublinia.ie

➕ 135 C8 ✉ St Michael's Hill, Christchurch
☎ 679 4611 ⏰ Apr–Sep daily 10–5; Oct–Mar, Mon–Sat 11–4, Sun and public hols 10–4.30
👆 Moderate (including Christ Church) 🍴 Tea room Jun–Aug (€) 🚌 Cross-city buses

GUINNESS STOREHOUSE

See pages 28–29.

HA'PENNY BRIDGE

This central Dublin landmark, originally called the Wellington Bridge after the Duke of Wellington, opened in 1816. It gained its nickname because up until 1919 it cost a half penny to go over the bridge. Before the opening of the new Millennium Bridge

in 2000 it was the only pedestrian bridge across the Liffey. The ornate, arched footbridge was renovated in 2001 and repainted its historically correct off-white. Three lamps supported by carved ironwork span the walkway which, together with the old-fashioned lampposts at either end, make the bridge particularly attractive when illuminated at night.

✠ 136 B2 ✉ Between Liffey Street Lower (north side) and Crown Alley (south side) 🚇 Tara Street 🚌 Cross-city buses

IRISH JEWISH MUSEUM

The earliest reference to Jewish people in Ireland records the arrival of five Jews from 'over the sea' in 1079, but the first to settle here came from Portugal and Spain at the end of the 15th century, fleeing persecution and the Inquisition. The former synagogue in which this museum is housed retains many of its original features. The museum traces the history and the cultural, professional and commercial life of Dublin's small but active Jewish community. It also chronicles Jewish lives through paintings, books and photographs, and has a re-created kitchen scene showing a typical Sabbath meal from the early 1900s.

✠ 135 F8 (off map) ✉ Walworth Road ☎ 453 1797 🕐 May–Sep Tue, Thu, Sun 11–3.30; Oct–Apr Sun 10.30–2.30 ✋ Free 🚌 16, 16A, 19, 19A

IRISH MUSEUM OF MODERN ART

The magnificent Royal Hospital building that houses the Irish Museum of Modern Art was designed by Sir William Robinson in 1684 for the Duke of Ormonde as a home for retired soldiers and was based on Les Invalides in Paris. It remained a home until 1927, and was finally restored in the 1980s. In 1991 it opened as the Irish Museum of Modern Art. Its stark grey-and-white interior provides a striking backdrop for the permanent collection of Irish and international modern and contemporary art. There are regular temporary exhibitions and a community programme covering music and the visual arts.

www.imma.ie

🏛 134 C2 ✉ Royal Hospital, Military Road, Kilmainham ☎ 612 9900
🕐 Tue–Sat 10–5.30, Sun and public hols 12–5.30 🍴 Café (€) 🚌 51B, 78A, 79, 90; tram LUAS 👋 Free; guided tours of the North Range: moderate
↔ Kilmainham Gaol (➤ 32–33) ❓ Formal gardens; bookshop

KILMAINHAM GAOL

See pages 32–33.

MARSH'S LIBRARY

Ireland's oldest public library has remained virtually unchanged throughout its 300-year history. There are some 25,000 volumes dating from the 15th to early 18th century, plus manuscripts and maps. At the far end of the reading gallery are three alcoves, or 'cages', where scholars were locked in to stop them from stealing valuable tomes. The oldest book is Cicero's *Letters to his Friends*, published in 1472, and other highlights are signed copies of books by Jonathan Swift and English poet John Donne. Signatures in the guest book include those of James Joyce and Daniel O'Connell.

www.marshlibrary.ie

🏛 135 E8 ✉ St Patrick's Close ☎ 454 3511 🕐 Mon, Wed, Thu, Fri 10–1, Sat 10.30–1 🚌 Cross-city buses 👋 Inexpensive

ST AUDOEN'S CHURCHES

The two churches dedicated to St Audoen – originally known as St Ouen – bishop of Rouen and patron saint of Normandy, stand side by side in the heart of the old medieval city. The most interesting is the Protestant St Audoen's, the only surviving medieval parish church in Dublin. It is believed there has been a church here since the 9th century, but the tower and door of this version dates from the 12th century. The nave was added in the 15th century and three of the bells date from 1423. Look for the restored memorials to the Sparke and Duff families. An exhibition explaining the importance of St Audoen's in the life of medieval Dublin is on display in the Guild Chapel of St Anne. The adjoining Roman Catholic Church of St Audoen was built between 1841 and 1847.

✚ 135 C7 ✉ Cornmarket, High Street ☎ 677 0088 🕐 Daily 9.30–5.30 (no admission after 4.45) 👆 Inexpensive 🚌 Cross-city buses

ST PATRICK'S CATHEDRAL

See pages 38–39.

SHAW'S BIRTHPLACE

'Author of many plays' is the simple accolade on the plaque outside the birthplace of George Bernard Shaw, the famous playwright. This restored Victorian home, close to the Grand Canal, reflects the life of a 19th-century middle-class family and was a source of inspiration for many of the characters Shaw would use later in his plays. You can see the drawing room where Shaw's mother held her musical soirees, the front parlour and the children's bedrooms. Shaw was born here in 1856, leaving 20 years later to live in London.

➕ 136 F1 ✉ 33 Synge Street ☎ 475 0854 🕐 May–Sep Mon–Tue, Thu–Fri 10–1, 2–5, Sat–Sun and public hols 2–5 🚌 16, 16A, 19, 19A, 122 ♿ Expensive ↔ Grand Canal (➤ 66)

SUNLIGHT CHAMBERS

On the corner of Essex Quay and Parliament Street, on the south side of the river, stands Sunlight Chambers. It was built at the turn of the 20th century as the Dublin offices of soap manufacturers Lever Brothers by Liverpool architect Edward Ould, who also designed Port Sunlight in England. The building has unusual Italianate terracotta friezes that advertise the company's product. In fact, they depict the history of hygiene. In its early years the building was unpopular because a 'foreign' architect had been employed, and upon its completion a journal called *The Irish Builder* referred to it as the 'ugliest building in Dublin'.

➕ 136 C1 ✉ Essex Quay 🕐 View from outside only 🚌 Cross-city buses

TEMPLE BAR

The area known as Temple Bar is sandwiched between Dame Street and the River Liffey and covers some 11ha (27 acres). Its origins can be traced back to Anglo-Irish Sir William Temple, who bought the land bounding the river in the 16th century and who liked to promenade with his family by the river. The word 'bar' means riverside path. The area gradually fell into decline as the shallow depth of the Liffey forced the docks area eastwards and Temple Bar sank into decay, its dark alleys harbouring the poorest citizens of Ireland. In the late 1970s, the land was acquired by Ireland's state transport company CIE, which had plans to build a huge bus depot on the site. While plans were being discussed the company rented out some of the derelict properties to artists, musicians and artisans.

In the 1980s, the residents and artists formed a lobbying group and set about trying to save Temple Bar, fighting for the preservation of the buildings in the area. The Irish government supported the cause and an organization called Temple Bar Properties was created to co-ordinate and administer the project; their information centre opened in early 2004. The progress made in the 1990s was staggering. This is now the cultural centre of the

city and the place to go for shopping, socializing, eating and drinking. The public open-air spaces, such as Meeting House Square, showcase Irish artistic talent, be it art, music or juggling. Streets a little further afield have also been brought under the Temple Bar umbrella, such as Cow's Lane, with its design shops, which has been redeveloped and pedestrianized.

Temple Bar has been almost too successful for its own good – with the stag and hen party revellers spilling out from the bars and restaurants, the residents and corporation believed the area was losing its way and gaining a reputation for over indulgence and drunken debauchery. It still gets a bit rowdy on the weekends for some, but during the day and weekday nights it's a great place to be. Among the principal arts venues are the Temple Bar Music Centre, the National Photographic Archive, Gallery of Photography, Temple Bar Gallery and Studios and The Ark.

www.templebar.ie

✚ 136 B2 🚉 Tara Street 🚌 Cross-city buses

Temple Bar Information Centre

✉ 12 East Essex Street, Temple Bar 🕐 Mon–Fri 9–5.30 (also Jun–Sep Sat 10–6, Sun 12.30–4.30)

WAR MEMORIAL GARDENS

These gardens are well off the tourist track, on the southern bank of the River Liffey opposite Phoenix Park. They are dedicated to the memory of the 49,400 Irish soldiers who died in World War I. The names of all the soldiers are contained in the two granite book rooms at either end of the gardens. Designed by the celebrated architect Sir Edwin

Lutyens, this moving place is well worth a visit. With herbaceous borders, sunken rose gardens and extensive tree planting, the gardens are enjoyable at any time of year.

134 C1 (off map) Islandbridge 677 0236
Mon–Fri 8–dusk, Sat–Sun 10–dusk Pearse
25, 25A, 51, 66, 66A, 66B, 69 Free
Kilmainham Gaol (➤ 32–33), Phoenix Park (➤ 97)

WHITEFRIAR STREET CARMELITE CHURCH AND ST VALENTINE'S SHRINE

This church is run by the Carmelite order, which returned from abroad in 1827 to re-establish a church in the city. There had been a priory on the site when it was seized during the Reformation in the 16th century. One of the best-loved churches in Dublin, it contains the relics of St Valentine, the patron saint of lovers. Valentine died in Rome, but his remains were finally returned to his native Ireland in 1836 as a gift from Pope Gregory XVI, in recognition of the preaching of the Irish Carmelite John Spratt. The casket containing his bones is kept in a shrine to the right of the high altar, and couples come here to pray, with special blessing services held on the saint's feast day, 14 February. Note the unusual oak statue of the Virgin (Our Lady of Dublin), the only surviving wooden statue from the sacking of Ireland's monasteries during the Reformation.

136 D1 56 Aungier Street 475 8821
Coffee shop (€) Mon, Wed–Fri 7.45am–6pm, Tue 7.45am–9.15pm, Sat–Sun 7.45am–7.30pm. Closed pm on public hols Pearse Cross-city buses Free

a walk through Viking and medieval Dublin

From Dublin Castle (➤ 24–25) go up the hill and turn left into Castle Street. At the end, go left into Werburgh Street; St Werburgh's Church is on the left.

The 18th-century church, named after the King of Mercia's daughter, was built on late 12th-century foundations.

Continue down until you see St Patrick's Cathedral (➤ 38–39) on your right. Cross the road and pass the cathedral on your right. Turn right into Kevin Street Upper; on the right is the Garda Station, site of the Episcopal Palace of St Sepulchre. Bear right into St Patrick's Close, with its medieval horse trough.

There are great views on all sides of St Patrick's Cathedral.

Turn right up Patrick Street and head towards Christ Church Cathedral (➤ 22–23). Walk right around the perimeter of the cathedral and follow the cobbled lane at the back across into Cross Lane South; on the left is Dvblinia (➤ 48). Turn right into St Michael's Close and left into Cook Street. On your left is St Audoen's arch (1240), leading to St Audoen's churches (➤ 52). Continue and go right into Bridge Street Lower.

On the left is the Brazen Head, known as the oldest pub in Dublin.

At the bridge, the site of the first Viking crossing, turn right into Merchant's Quay and then second right into Fishamble Street.

Copper Alley, up the hill on the left (running through the Harding Hotel), was one of the earliest Viking streets.

Continue to the top and turn left into Lord Edward Street, which filters into Dame Street; opposite City Hall is the Queen of Tarts.

Distance 3km (2 miles)
Time 2 hours
Start point Dublin Castle, Dame Street ✛ 136 C1
End point City Hall, Dame Street ✛ 136 C1
Lunch Queen of Tarts

Southside East

Stately Georgian architecture, a cluster of outstanding national museums, a famous university and some of the best shopping in Ireland are all located in this area. There is so much to do and see in this relatively compact part of the city that just walking around and taking in all the colours, sounds and contrasts is quite an experience.

Grafton Street is the hub of the shopping area, a traditional (though pedestrianized) street scene, full of people and dotted with all kinds of street performers, with a glittering modern shopping centre at one end. Narrow side streets are a colourful mix of smaller shops, cafés and pubs, and surrounding streets have

interesting individual shops and classy designer boutiques. Nearby you can wander into the peaceful haven of Trinity College and discover the treasures of its old library, or visit the National Museum, Natural History Museum or National Gallery, next door to the parliament buildings of Leinster House. Further south is a concentration of fine Georgian architecture around leafy Merrion and Fitzwilliam squares, and the lovely St Stephen's Green, an oasis of calm in the heart of the city. Take afternoon tea at the historic Shelbourne Hotel to complete the central Dublin experience.

BALLSBRIDGE

This leafy suburb was laid out mainly in the mid-19th century but it still retains some grand Georgian houses making it an exclusive and expensive place to live. It is sometimes known as the Embassy district, as foreign consulates have taken up residence here, along with smart hotels and the Royal Dublin Society Showgrounds, where prestigious events are held, such as the Dublin Horse Show. Close to the Lansdowne Road DART station is the Irish national rugby stadium, another Ballsbridge landmark.

✚ 137 F7 (off map) ✉ Southeast of city centre 🚉 Lansdowne Road 🚌 5, 7, 7A, 18, 45, 46, 84

BANK OF IRELAND

The bank began life as the upper and lower houses of the old Irish Parliament in 1739, the first purpose-built parliament buildings in Europe. The House of Commons was destroyed by fire in 1792,

but the House of Lords remains intact and can be visited. The Act of Union of 1800 shifted direct rule to London and the parliament buildings, on becoming vacant, were purchased by the Bank of Ireland in 1802. The House of Lords has a fine vaulted ceiling and oak panelling, a sparkling Waterford crystal chandelier and huge tapestries depicting the 1689 siege at Londonderry and the 1690 battle of the Boyne. Going through the Foster Place entrance you can visit the Bank of Ireland Arts Centre, which features an exhibition, the 'Story of Banking'. The mace, made in 1765, was retained despite the British Government's insistence that all traces of the Irish House of Commons were removed. The centre also hosts lunchtime concerts and a range of evening cultural events.

🚹 136 C2 ✉ 2 College Green ☎ 677 6801 🕐 House of Lords: Mon, Tue, Fri 10–4, Wed 10.30–4, Thu 10–5. Bank of Ireland Arts Centre: Tue–Fri 10–4 🚉 Tara Street 🚌 Cross-city buses ♿ Free; arts centre inexpensive

BEWLEY'S ORIENTAL CAFÉ

This café is a Dublin institution and worth visiting for the ambience alone. The family connection goes back to the 1840s when Joshua Bewley set up as a tea merchant. His son Ernest opened the first branch in South Great George's Street (now closed) in 1894. He introduced coffee and his wife baked scones and cakes. As the cafés grew in popularity, the family opened the now famous Grafton Street branch in 1927. Here you can sip coffee or eat a meal in the upstairs restaurant amid the original art-nouveau and art-deco features. This is where writers including Brendan Behan and Patrick Kavanagh came during the 1950s. On the first floor, in the former chocolate factory, there is a small museum displaying family portraits, old equipment and early teapots. The Bewley business has continued to expand, with further cafés in Waterstones bookshops and a contemporary café in Dublin airport.

🚹 136 D2 ✉ 78 Grafton Street ☎ 679 4085 🕐 Mon–Thu 7.30am–11pm, Fri–Sat 7.30am–1am, Sun 8am–11pm 🚉 Tara Street 🚌 Cross-city buses ↔ Trinity College (➤ 40–41), Bank of Ireland (➤ above)

DUBLIN CITY LIBRARY AND ARCHIVE

Dublin City Library, re-opened in July 2003 after major refurbishment, offers all the usual facilities of a lending library, plus a business information facility and music library. Of most interest to visitors are the excellent Dublin City Archive and Dublin & Irish Local Studies Collections. These archives contain the records of Dublin's civic government since 1171 and give a vivid picture of the city over eight centuries. In the local studies section there is a fascinating collection of books, newspapers, photographs, maps, prints, theatre programmes, posters, ballad sheets and audio-visual material giving a unique insight into the city of Dublin. You can look through the local parish records and trace your family history if you have Irish ancestors, although the main centre of genealogical studies is at the National Library (➤ 72–73) in Kildare Street. There is also a 100-seat Public Reading room and a café.
www.dublincity.ie/living_in_the_city/libraries
✚ 137 C5 ✉ 138–144 Pearse Street ☎ 674 4800 ◷ Mon–Thu 10–8, Fri–Sat 10–5 ▨ Free ⬛ Pearse ▤ 2, 3

FITZWILLIAM SQUARE

This is one of Dublin's most famous squares. The first house was built here in 1714, which means the square's architecture spans the reigns of all four Georgian kings. The central garden is private and only the residents hold keys. The artist Jack B Yeats (1871–1957), who lived at No 18, is among the illustrious people to have resided here. There is plenty of Georgian detail, including original fanlights, and on some houses a box-shaped recess that held the lamps. Look, too, for original door knockers and elaborate iron foot-scrapers. Some houses have spikes set into the wall beside the windows, installed to deter 19th-century burglars, and

there are examples of ornamental iron balconies and attractive metal coal-hole covers.

✚ 136 F4 🚌 Cross-city buses 🖐 Free

GRAFTON STREET

Dublin's most popular thoroughfare is only 200m (650ft) long and 6m (20ft) wide. This attractive pedestrianized street, linking Trinity College and St Stephen's Green, is lined with four-storey Georgian buildings, and together with some of the smaller alleyways off the street, houses a selection of Dublin's best shops, restaurants, cafés – especially Bewley's (➤ 63) – pubs and bars. Flower sellers and street musicians add to this attractive city scene.

✚ 136 D2 ✉ Grafton Street 🚉 Tara Street/Pearse 🚌 Cross-city buses

GRAND CANAL

Canals were the innovative form of cargo transport in the 18th century and Dublin's Grand Canal and Royal Canal were no exception. The Grand Canal crossed Leinster from Dublin to the River Shannon in Offaly, with a branch south to join the lovely River Barrow. Some 6km (4 miles) of the canal loops around Dublin, though it has carried no commercial traffic since the early 1960s. It's a pleasant place to stroll or take a boat trip, and is a haven for wildlife. At Grand Canal Quay, a few minutes' walk from the DART city station, is the Waterways Visitor Centre (➤ 79), which houses an interactive multimedia exhibition of Ireland's inland waterways. It forms part of the quay's ambitious development project, which will include a new marina, apartments and offices. A good two-hour walk along the towpath takes you all the way to Kilmainham. You can rest on the bench near Baggot Street Bridge, next to the bronze statue of poet Patrick Kavanagh (1905–67), who loved this stretch of water.

✚ 137 F5 ✉ Grand Canal Quay 🚇 Grand Canal Dock 🚌 2, 3

HERALDIC MUSEUM

The Heraldic Museum has been attached to the Office of the Chief Herald since 1909 and is an integral part of the National Library. It is housed in an attractive 19th-century building, the former Kildare Street Club, designed by Benjamin Woodward. Interesting carvings on the exterior include monkeys playing billiards and decorative birds. In the main exhibition room you can see the modern banners of Ireland's ancient chieftain families, creating a colourful display, along with paintings, Belleek pottery and shields. Note the colours of the Irish infantry regiments that fought in France during the 18th century. From further afield are the arms of Napoleon, Sir Francis Drake and the Spencer-Churchill family. The museum also traces the origins of heraldry both in Ireland and throughout Europe.

www.nli.ie

🞖 136 D4 ✉ 2 Kildare Street ☎ 603 0311
🕐 Mon–Wed 10–8, Thu–Fri 10–4.30, Sat 10–12.30 ✋ Free 🚇 Pearse 🚌 Cross-city buses ↔ National Library (➤ 72–73), National Gallery (➤ 34–35), National Museum (➤ 36–37)

IVEAGH HOUSE AND GARDENS

Iveagh House was donated to the state by Sir Robert Guinness, 2nd Earl of Iveagh, in 1939. Originally two houses when built in the 1760s, the Guinness family bought the properties in the 1860s and linked them under a stone façade, incorporating the family arms on the pediment. They subsequently altered the interior to include a new ballroom with an impressive domed ceiling. The house is now used by the Department of Foreign Affairs and is not open to the public. Hidden beyond Iveagh House are the lovely, secluded Iveagh Gardens. This is one of Dublin's finest but least well known parks, just south of St Stephen's Green and entered by a small side street, Clonmel Street. Designed in 1863 by Ninian Niven, it includes a central area with lawns, statues and fountains echoing the Bois de Boulogne in Paris. Other areas have a more natural feel with a rustic grotto, woodlands and wilderness. There is also a maze and archery lawn reminiscent of Hampton Court in London. It's the perfect place to escape the hectic city on a warm summer's day.

🞖 136 E3 ✉ Clonmel Street ☎ 475 7816 🕐 Mar–Oct Mon–Sat 8–6, Sun and public hols 10–6; Nov–Feb Mon–Sat 8–4. Sun and public hols 10–4
✋ Free 🚌 Cross-city buses

a walk around Dublin's Pubs

Begin at the Stag's Head in Dame Court, a small road off Dame Lane. Walk south to Exchequer Street and turn left. Continue to the Old Stand, one of Dublin's oldest pubs, on the left. Opposite, on the corner of Wicklow Street, is the International Bar. Turn right into William Street South and leave Powerscourt Shopping Centre on your left; opposite is Grogan's.

Grogan's has long been popular with writers and artists.

Continue towards the end of the street, turning left into Chatham Row and into Chatham Street; Victorian-style Neary's is on your right. Turn left into Grafton Street and next left into Harry Street for McDaid's. Return to Grafton Street and go straight across to Anne Street South; halfway down is the John Kehoe.

Kehoe's is an excellent example of a traditional old-style pub with plenty of *craic*.

Continue along Anne Street South and turn left into Dawson Street; take the next left into Duke Street to Davy Byrnes, a former haunt of James Joyce. Continue on and turn right into Grafton Street; take the second left into Suffolk Street. Follow the road round into Church Lane where you will find O'Neill's, a popular student watering hole, on the corner. Follow the road round and turn left into Dame Street. Cross the road and take the first right into Anglesea Street. At the end is the Oliver St John Gogarty on the right and the Auld Dubliner on the left. Turn left into Temple Bar (➤ 55–56).

There are numerous pubs, bars and eating places here, including the Temple Bar, with its beer garden.

Distance 1.5km (1 mile)
Time Depends how thirsty you are
Start point Stag's Head, Dame Court  136 B2
End point The Temple Bar, 33–34 Temple Bar 136 B2
Lunch Good choice of pubs, restaurants and cafés in Temple Bar

LEINSTER HOUSE

This is one of Dublin's finest Georgian town houses, built in 1745 for the Earl of Kildare.

It was renamed when the Earl became Duke of Leinster in 1766. The building eventually passed to the government and in 1922, with the forming of the Irish Free State, it became the head-quarters of the new government. Today it is the seat of the Oireachtas (parliament) and houses the Dáil (lower house) and the Seannad (upper house or Senate).

✚ 136 D4 ✉ Kildare Street ☎ 618 3166 🕐 Call for information ✋ Free
🍴 Café (€) 🚉 Pearse 🚌 Cross-city buses ❓ Visits by tour only, 2 hours

MERRION SQUARE

Languishing on a rock on the edge of Merrion Square's central park is a superb statue of Oscar Wilde. The author lived at No 1 between 1855 and 1876, and his house is a fine example of the city's Georgian architecture. Merrion is one of Dublin's most prestigious squares, laid out in 1762, and bordered by Leinster House, the National Gallery, the Natural History Museum and numerous smaller examples of Georgian splendour. Here you will find town houses with wrought-iron balconies, brightly painted doors, fanlights and elaborate door-knockers. The learned and the illustrious have lived here, including W B Yeats and the Duke of Wellington. Just off the square is Number Twenty-Nine (➤ 75), a Georgian gem. The park is a delightful place to be on a sunny day, with its outstanding array of seasonal floral displays. Every Saturday and Sunday (10–6.30) there is an art display in the park.

✚ 137 D5 ✉ Merrion Square 🕐 Park: daylight hours only 🚉 Pearse
🚌 Cross-city buses

NATIONAL GALLERY

See pages 34–35.

NATIONAL LIBRARY

The library opened in 1890 in a late 19th-century Renaissance-style building, designed by Sir Thomas Deane. It was originally built to house the collection of the Royal Dublin Society, the institution concerned with the implementation of Dublin's national museums and galleries. The National Library contains the world's largest collection of Irish documentary material: books, manuscripts, newspapers, periodicals, drawings, photographs and maps. Its mission is to collect and preserve these documents and to make them available to the public. It does not lend them out and all research has to take place in the reading rooms. The domed reading room on the first floor is particularly magnificent, and

luminaries such as James Joyce worked here. You will need to get a reader's ticket to access any information, but it is free to look around. The library is most visited for its Genealogy Service (Mon–Fri 10–4.45, Sat 10–12.30) and family history research. There is a huge resource of Catholic parish records, 19th-century land valuations, trade and social directories, estate records and the largest collection of newspapers in Ireland, containing the all-important Births, Deaths and Marriages columns. The office of the Chief Herald and the Heraldic Museum (➤ 66–67) are also within the library. The huge collection of the National Photographic Archive has now moved to Temple Bar (➤ 55–56).
www.nli.ie

✠ 136 D4 ✉ Kildare Street ☎ 603 0200 🕐 Mon–Wed 10–9, Thu–Fri 10–5, Sat 10–1 ✋ Free 🚉 Pearse 🚌 Cross-city buses ↔ Heraldic Museum (➤ 66–67); National Gallery (➤ 34–35); National Museum (➤ 36–37)

NATIONAL MUSEUM
See pages 36–37.

NATIONAL PRINT MUSEUM
An idiosyncratic little museum in a former soldiers' chapel houses a unique collection of objects related to the printing industry in Ireland. Much of the machinery is still in full working order. Guided tours make this a much more fun experience than it sounds. The processes of printing, from Gutenburg's Bible of 1455 through to the political printed material of the Easter Rising of 1916, are documented and the various methods of production and bookbinding explained. The guides, some of them retired printers, are very knowledgeable. Upstairs the walls are adorned with newspapers, showing the different styles of printed presentation and recalling major historic events in Ireland.

✠ 137 F7 ✉ Garrison Chapel, Beggar's Bush, Haddington Road ☎ 660 3770 🕐 Mon–Fri 10–5. Closed public hols. Some weekend opening, check for details 🍴 Coffee shop (€) 🚉 Grand Canal Dock 🚌 7, 7A, 45 ✋ Moderate

NATURAL HISTORY MUSEUM

For an original Victorian experience look no further than Dublin's fascinating Natural History Museum. It may be known as the city's 'Dead Zoo', but it gives a unique insight into the way Victorians treated the study and display of animals, and the values that went with that. You won't find interactives or touch-screen technology here; instead you will find antique displays showing some 10,000 stuffed animals – drawn from a collection of around 2 million specimens. Some of them are in poor shape, while others are being replaced. The ground floor is devoted to Irish animals, including skeletons of the huge, extinct Irish deer or elk, complete with impressive antlers. The upper two floors display animals, birds, fish, reptiles, insects and invertebrates from around the world. A huge 20m (65ft) long skeleton of a humpback whale is suspended from the ceiling and there is the skeleton of the fascinating but sadly extinct dodo.
www.museum.ie

✚ 136 D4 ✉ Merrion Street ☎ 677 7444 ◑ Tue–Sat 10–5, Sun 2–5 ⊠ Pearse ▣ Cross-city buses ✋ Free
↔ National Gallery (➤ 34–35)

NEWMAN HOUSE

This is in fact two houses, both of them among the finest Georgian houses in Dublin. Cardinal Newman used the mansion in the 1850s to launch his great experiment to bring education to the Catholic Masses. The Catholic University of Ireland was established here in 1865 and provided further education for men such as James Joyce and Eamon de Valera, who did not wish to attend the Protestant Trinity College. Newman House remains part of the original University, now known as University College Dublin. The houses are of interest for their spectacular plasterwork and superlative 18th-century interiors. Number 85 has work by Switzerland's great Lafranchini brothers, who decorated the walls and ceilings.

➕ 136 E2 ✉ 85–86 St Stephen's Green ☎ 716 7422 🕐 Jun–Aug Tue–Fri, tours at 12, 2, 3 and 4 ✋ Moderate 🚇 Pearse 🚌 Cross-city buses ❓ Guided tours only ↔ University Church (➤ 79)

NUMBER TWENTY NINE

Beautifully restored Number Twenty Nine is one of Dublin's Georgian jewels. It is laid out as the home of a middle-class family between 1790 and 1820, and offers a rare insight into the life of the period. An audio-visual show at the start of the tour introduces you to the family members, then leads from the servants' quarters in the basement to the attic playroom. Throughout are original artefacts and furnishings of the period, all recapturing the spirit of the age. It is the everyday items, in addition to some wonderful paintings, furnishings and plasterwork, that really bring this home to life.

➕ 137 E5 ✉ 29 Fitzwilliam Street Lower ☎ 702 6165 🕐 Tue–Sat 10–5, Sun 2–5 ✋ Moderate 🍴 Tea room 🚇 Pearse 🚌 7, 10A, 13A ↔ National Gallery (➤ 34–35)

OSCAR WILDE'S HOUSE

The home of writer Oscar Wilde from 1855 to 1876 is an excellent example of Georgian architecture. The restored house, on the north side of Merrion Square (➤ 71), with its remarkable cornices and architraves, was the first to be built on the square in 1762. In 1994 the American College Dublin took over the house and opened it for guided tours. Renovation involved the revival of traditional crafts to repair the plasterwork and restore the original stone and wooden floors. Use of period paints, antique furnishings and reproduction Georgian furniture have given a first-class result.
www.amcd.edu

✚ 136 D4 ✉ 1 Merrion Square ☎ 662 0281 ⊙ Mon, Wed, Thu tours at 10.15 and 11.15 ✋ Inexpensive 🚊 Pearse 🚌 Cross-city buses ⬌ National Gallery (➤ 34–35), National Library (➤ 72–73)

ROYAL COLLEGE OF SURGEONS

This internationally renowned institution is in one of the city's best Georgian buildings, overlooking St Stephen's Green (➤ 78). It dates from 1806 and has a neoclassical granite façade and distinctive round-headed windows. The three statues above the pediment are of Hygieia (goddess of health), Asclepius (god of medicine) and Athena (goddess of wisdom). The building was commandeered by Irish Volunteers under the leadership of Countess Markievicz in the 1916 Easter Rising, and you can still see the bullet marks on the façade.

✚ 136 E2 ✉ 123 St Stephen's Green ☎ 402 2248 ⊙ By appointment only ✋ Free 🚊 Pearse Street 🚌 Cross-city buses ❓ Guided tours on request

ST ANN'S CHURCH

For the best view of this striking church, founded in 1707, look down Anne Street South from Grafton Street. The church was created for the rapidly evolving Georgian suburbs occupied by wealthy and influential residents. Its stunning Romanesque façade was added in 1868 by architects Deane and Woodward. Inside is a series of colourful stained-glass windows dating from the mid-19th century. It was here that the 18th-century nationalist leader Wolfe Tone was married in 1785, as was Bram Stoker, the author of *Dracula*, in 1878. St Ann's has a long tradition of charity work; in 1723 Baron Butler left a bequest to provide 120 loaves of bread each week for the poor, and today anyone may take a loaf from the shelf beside the altar.

✝ 136 D3 ✉ Dawson Street
☎ 676 7727 🕐 Mon–Fri 10–4
and Sunday service 👋 Free
🚉 Pearse Street
🚌 Cross-city buses

ST STEPHEN'S GREEN

This pleasant park is one of the most famous in central Dublin. Once common ground where public hangings, whippings and burnings took place, today the 9ha (22-acre) green is a popular lunchtime venue for office and shop workers and a haven for visitors when sightseeing gets a bit too much. The duck pond, attractive flower beds and beautiful garden for the blind create a sanctuary from the city. The green was landscaped in the 18th century and St Stephen's became much sought after by the wealthy, who began to build their glorious Georgian town houses around the central park. Trees and paths, railings and gates were installed and you could have access to the green at an annual cost of one guinea. The public were allowed free access again following an act of parliament proposed by Sir Arthur Guinness in 1877. The north side, known as Beaux Walk in the 18th-century, is still the most fashionable part, overlooked by the exclusive Shelbourne hotel. Highlights are the Fusliers' Arch at the Grafton Street entrance, the Three Fates Fountain and the modern memorial, near Merrion Row, to the nationalist Wolfe Tone, better known locally as Tonehenge. Notable buildings around the green include the Royal College of Surgeons (➤ 76) and Newman House (➤ 75).

✚ 136 D3 ✉ Top of Grafton Street ⊙ Mon–Sat 8–dusk, Sun, public hols 10–dusk ✋ Free 🚇 Pearse 🚌 Cross-city buses

TRINITY COLLEGE AND THE BOOK OF KELLS

See pages 40–41.

UNIVERSITY CHURCH

It's easy to miss the front entrance to this church, which is next door to Newman House in St Stephen's Green. If you can find it, beyond the small entrance porch is a remarkable Byzantine-style interior. Commissioned by Cardinal Newman in 1856, the church was built on the garden plot between No 86 and No 87. The nave is richly decorated with Irish marble slabs and there is an ornate canopy over the altar. Look for the little birds on the capitals of the columns dividing the marble panels. John Hungerford Pollen, architect and friend of Newman, came over from England to supervise the building and also painted the elaborate ceiling. The lighting is subdued, the church lit by small windows set under the roof, and the whole atmosphere is one of calm and tranquillity.

✚ 136 E2 ✉ 87A St Stephen's Green ☎ 478 1606 🕓 Mon–Sat 9–5.30, Sun 10–1, 5–6 💷 Free 🚉 Pearse 🚌 Cross-city buses ↔ Newman House (➤ 75)

WATERWAYS VISITOR CENTRE

This centre, at Grand Canal Quay, is known to locals as 'the box

in the docks' because of its distinct shape. It recounts the 200 years of the Grand's transition from its original use as a commercial waterway to its present-day recreational role using working models, audiovisual displays and information panels. It also includes examples of art and literature inspired by the waterways. A new marina is being built close to the centre.

✚ 137 D7 ✉ Waterways Visitor Centre: Grand Canal Quay ☎ 677 7510 🕓 Jun–Sep daily 9.30–5.30; Oct–May Wed–Sun 12.30–5 💷 Inexpensive 🚉 Grand Canal Dock 🚌 2, 3

Northside

Long overshadowed by the Southside, this part of the city has always had a unique character – more workaday and down to earth, but with such gems as the Dublin Writers Museum, the renowned Abbey and Gate theatres and, of course, the splendid central thoroughfare of O'Connell Street. Today, things are a little different north of the river, with the rejuvenation of the Smithfield and dockland areas bringing a trendy cachet to the whole scene.

O'Connell Street is still the hub, a wide street where shops, hotels and fast-food outlets are anchored by the impressive and historic General Post Office, famous for the role it played in the 1916 Easter Rising. Opposite the GPO is the soaring, slender Spire, erected in 2002. The southern end is presided over by a great statue of Daniel O'Connell, then comes O'Connell Bridge and the River Liffey. East along the river stands the imposing Custom House, while the quays to the west lead to the Four Courts, a superlative National Museum of Decorative Arts and History, housed in the former Collins Barracks, and the glorious Phoenix Park.

This is a fascinating part of the city to explore, with its mix of earthy street markets, lofty cultural establishments, trendy bars, statues and monuments, and parks and gardens.

ABBEY THEATRE

The Irish National Theatre was founded in 1903 by W B Yeats and Lady Augusta Gregory. Premises were purchased in Abbey Street and the theatre was first opened to the public on 27 December, 1904. In its early days there were riots after performances of plays by playwrights such as Sean O'Casey. Following a fire in 1951, the Abbey remained closed until 1966. The Peacock Theatre was incorporated in the basement with the prime object of showcasing new plays by burgeoning Irish writers. Established writers, including Brian Friel and Hugh Leonard, have their new works premièred here, and classic plays, such as *The Playboy of the Western World* by J M Synge, are regularly produced.

www.abbeytheatre.ie

✚ 136 A3 ✉ 26 Abbey Street Lower
☎ 878 7222 🕐 Peformances Mon–Sat 8pm, Sat matinees 2.30; Peacock Theatre: Mon–Sat 8.15pm, Sat matinees 2.45
✋ Expensive, varies according to performance 🚇 Tara Street, Connolly, Abbey LUAS 🚌 Cross-city buses
❓ Backstage tours on Thu ☎ 887 7223
↔ General Post Office (➤ 26–27), Custom House (➤ 86–87)

BLESSINGTON STREET BASIN

Now known as Dublin's 'secret garden', Blessington is only 10 minutes' walk from O'Connell Street. The Basin was originally constructed around 1803 to provide a reservoir for the city's water supply. In the 1860s it was used exclusively to provide water to

two distilleries – Jamesons in Bow Street and Powers in John's Lane – and this continued until the 1970s. The Basin was completely refurbished in 1994 and is now a peaceful haven for visitors and local residents, and a safe environment for wildlife.

⊞ 132 E2 ⊠ Blessington Street ☎ Dublin Parks 661 2369 ◐ Dawn–dusk
🚌 10A

THE BRAM STOKER DRACULA EXPERIENCE

Bram Stoker, author of the famous novel *Dracula* (1897), was born in the seaside suburb of Clontarf. This museum, dedicated to him, opened in 2003 at a cost of over €2 million. It covers an area of 929sq m (10,000sq ft) and makes use of all the latest technology. The 'Time Tunnel to Transylvania' transports you to the depths of Count Dracula's castle, to the Blood Laboratory and Renfield's Lunatic Asylum; not for the faint-hearted. There is also a section devoted to Stoker's life and his literary achievements.

www.thebramstokerdraculaexperience.com

⊞ 133 D8 (off map) ⊠ Westwood Club, Clontarf Road ☎ 805 7824
◐ Fri–Sun 12–10 🍴 Restaurant, bar (€–€€) 🚩 Clontarf Road 🚌 27, 27B, 29A, 31, 32, 32A, 32B, 42, 42A, 42B, 43, 127, 129, 130

THE CASINO, MARINO

Although now surrounded by modern suburbia, the Casino ('small house') is one of the finest 18th-century neoclassical buildings in Ireland. George III's architect, Sir William Chambers, designed it along the lines of a Roman temple, and it contains 16 beautifully decorated rooms. It was built for James Caulfield, 1st Earl Charlemont, as a summer house where he could indulge his passion for all things Italian, following his Grand Tour of the Mediterranean. Throughout the rooms are fine ornamental plasterwork, exceptional parquet floors of rare woods, and practical features such as drainpipes hidden in ornate columns. The Casino was acquired by the state in 1930, after it had fallen into disrepair. Considerable restoration in the 1970s gradually returned it to its original condition, although work still continues.

✚ 133 D8 (off map) ✉ Off Malahide Road, Marino
☎ 833 1618 🕐 Jun–Sep daily 10–6; May, Oct daily 10–5; Apr Sat–Sun 12–5; Feb, Mar, Nov, Dec Sat–Sun 12–4. Last admission 50 mins before closing 🚻 Inexpensive 🚉 Clontarf Road 🚌 20A, 20B, 27, 27A, 27B, 42, 42C ❓ Visit by guided tour

COLLINS BARRACKS

One of the most impressive museum spaces in Europe, the former barracks now houses the National Museum of Decorative Arts and History and is the administrative headquarters of the National Museum of Ireland. It was built as the Royal Barracks in 1704, and was renamed Collins Barracks in memory of Republican hero Michael Collins, following Irish independence. In 1994 the barracks were assigned to the National Museum of Ireland and after extensive restoration now display some of the 250,000 artefacts that make up exhibits charting Ireland's economic, social, political and military progress. There is an awesome collection of silver, ceramics, glassware, weapons, furniture and costumes. Highlights include the rare 14th-century Fonthill Vase, 19th-century neo-Celtic furniture and costume and jewellery in 'The Way We Wore' exhibition. Don't miss the 'Curators' Choice' – 25 objects chosen by the curators of the various collections. Further developments will include more temporary exhibition space and galleries for ethnography and earth sciences displays.

www.museum.ie

🕂 135 B5 ✉ Benburb Street ☎ 677 7444 🕐 Tue–Sat 10–5, Sun 2–5 ♿ Free; guided tours inexpensive 🍴 Museum café (€) 🚆 Heuston LUAS 🚌 25, 25A, 66, 67, 90

CUSTOM HOUSE

The best view of this impressive Georgian building, just past Eden Quay, is from the south side of the River Liffey. The huge neoclassical Custom House – 114m (375ft) long – was designed by James Gandon in 1791 as the port of Dublin became increasingly more important to the city. The Act of Union of 1800 put paid to this as the custom and excise business moved to London and its role became redundant. Stretching along the waterfront, the main façade is made up of arched arcades with a Doric portico at its centre. It is topped by a green copper cupola or dome 38m (125ft) high with a 5m (16ft) statue of Commerce crowning the dome. Look for the frieze above the centre for a series of 14 allegorical heads that represent the 13 rivers of Ireland and the Atlantic Ocean. Other statues represent the four continents, while those of cattle emphasize Dublin's beef trade. The building suffered fire damage during one of the more dramatic events of 1921, although it was not completely destroyed, and restoration took place after the fire and again in the 1980s. The building now contains government offices and a Visitor Centre, complete with its Gandon Museum and a history of the Custom House.

➕ 136 A4 ✉ Custom House Quay ☎ 888 2538 🕐 Mid-Mar to Nov Mon–Fri 10–12.30, Sat–Sun 2–5; Nov to mid-Mar Wed–Fri 10–12.30, Sun 2–5 ✋ Inexpensive 🚉 Tara Street 🚌 Cross-city buses

DUBLIN WRITERS MUSEUM

The journalist and author Maurice Gorham (1902–75) was the first to propose the idea of this museum to Dublin Tourism. It was not, however, until 1991 that the museum finally came to fruition. Ireland has produced a staggering number of the world's greatest writers and where better to showcase their work than in this glorious 18th-century town house in central Dublin. The aim of the museum is to promote interest in Irish literature and, through its association with the Irish Writers' Centre next door, to encourage today's writers. The town house accommodates the museum rooms, library, gallery and offices, while an annexe behind houses the coffee shop, bookshop, and exhibition and lecture rooms.

Take the audio commentary that leads you through the displays, giving you the background story to Dublin's literary heritage. Displays include letters, manuscripts, paintings and personal belongings and memorabilia. The museum also has a room devoted to children's literature, and hosts regular readings and temporary exhibitions. Take a little time to view the building itself, with its exceptional stucco plasterwork and sumptuous furnishings.

➕ 132 E4 ✉ 18 Parnell Square North ☎ 872 2077 🕐 Jun–Aug Mon–Fri 10–6, Sat 10–5, Sun 11–5; Sep–May Mon–Sat 10–5, Sun and public hols 11–5 ✋ Expensive 🍴 Chapter One restaurant (€€; closed Sun–Mon) and café (€; closed Sun and public hols) 🚉 Connolly 🚌 Cross-city buses ❓ Self-guided audio tour (30 mins); combined ticket available with James Joyce Museum (➤ 121) and Shaw's Birthplace (➤ 53)

DUBLIN ZOO

Set in a beautifully landscaped area of Phoenix Park (➤ 97), Dublin
Zoo covers some 26ha (64 acres). It was founded in 1830 with
animals from London Zoo. The aim of the zoo has changed since
its early days, when the objective was to show people, who had
never seen the like before, as many different species as possible.
Today the zoo is concerned with conservation, education and
animal study and it is part of an important international programme
to breed and preserve endangered species, in particular the
golden lion tamarin and the Moluccan cockatoo. One of the latest
additions has been the African Plains, consisting of a large lake,
pasture land and mature woodland. The animals featured on the
plain include giraffes, hippos, rhinos, chimpanzees, lions, cheetahs
and ostriches. Take the Nakuru Safari, a 25-minute tour of the
African Plains, with full on-board commentary. Other highlights are
the World of Cats, the Fringes of the Arctic and the City Farm,
where children can handle pets and farm animals.

www.dublinzoo.ie

✚ 130 F3 ✉ Phoenix Park ☎ 677 1425 🕐 Mar–Sep Mon–Sat 9.30–6, Sun
10.30–6; Oct–Feb Mon–Sat 9.30–dusk, Sun 10.30–dusk. Last admission

one hour before closing. Nakuru Safari daily between 11 and 4
👜 Expensive; Nakuru Safari extra, moderate 🍴 Restaurant, cafés (€),
picnic areas 🚉 Heuston LUAS 🚌 10, 10A, 25, 26, 66, 66A, 66B,
67, 67A

FOUR COURTS

Four Courts was built by James Gandon
between 1786 and 1802. This huge
Georgian complex along the river is still
Ireland's main criminal court so you can
visit only when court is in session,
although you cannot enter the courts
and restricted areas. The building
suffered damage during the Civil War
and was not restored until the 1930s.

🔢 138 B8 ✉ Inns Quay 🚉 Four Courts LUAS
☎ 872 5555 🕐 Mon–Fri 10–1, 2–4 only when court is in session
👜 Free 🚌 Cross-city buses

GAA MUSEUM

The GAA Museum in Croke Park is the home of the Gaelic Athletic
Association (GAA), the governing body of Ireland's national sports
– essentially hurling and Gaelic football. The Irish are passionate
about these sports and about the stadium, which can hold 82,000
spectators and is always full to capacity for the All-Ireland finals.
The museum traces the history of the sports through interactive
touch screens and sporting memorabilia, and highlights the
personalities involved in the sports over the years. A tour of the
stadium (Apr–Sep 12.30 and 3pm; Oct–Mar 2pm) includes a look
behind the scenes as well as an opportunity to see the pitch.
www.gaa.ie

🔢 133 D6 ✉ Croke Park, St Joseph's Avenue ☎ 819 2323 🕐 Mon–Sat
9.30–5, Sun and public hols 12–5 (not open match days) 👜 Expensive
🍴 Coffee shop (€) 🚉 Connolly (15-min walk) 🚌 3, 11, 11A, 16, 16A

GATE THEATRE

Established in 1928, the Gate is housed in an elegant late-Georgian building. From the outset it offered Dublin audiences the best of international productions, as well as plays from the classic and contemporary Irish repertoire. Many famous names first performed at the Gate, including James Mason and a young Orson Welles. It also presents festivals of works by playwrights such as Harold Pinter and Samuel Beckett. Check the website for latest productions.

www.gate-theatre.ie

✚ 132 F4 ✉ 1 Cavendish Row, Parnell Square East
☎ 874 4085, box office 874 4045 🕐 Check for performance times, building open Mon–Sat 10–7
✋ Depends on performance 🚌 Cross-city buses

GENERAL POST OFFICE

See pages 26–27.

GLASNEVIN CEMETERY

This cemetery was established in 1832 by Daniel O'Connell when Catholics were at last legally allowed to conduct funerals. It is Ireland's largest cemetery (49ha/121 acres), and around 1.2 million people are buried here. There are ornately carved Celtic crosses, Gothic mausoleums and tombs of the famous. Join one of the free tours to discover who has been buried here in the last two centuries. The names are synonymous with Dublin and Ireland, both political and cultural. Charles Stewart Parnell, Michael Collins and Eamon de Valera – the latter a leader of the 1916 Easter Rising, who went on to be Taoiseach seven times

and President of Ireland twice – are among the famous political names. W B Yeats, Brendan Behan, the poet Gerard Manley Hopkins and the arts benefactor Alfred Chester Beatty lie here too. O'Connell is commemorated by a 51m (167ft) tall round tower. The pauper's graves are poignant reminders of the devastation wrought by famine and cholera in the 1840s.

www.glasnevin-cemetry.ie

✚ 131 A7 ✉ Finglas Road, Glasnevin ☎ 830 1133 🕓 Mon–Sat 8.30–4.30, Sun 9–4.30 ✋ Free 🚌 19, 40 ❓ Tours Wed, Fri 2.30; approx 2 hours

HUGH LANE GALLERY

Charlemont House in Parnell Square is the perfect setting for the fine collection of modern art bequeathed to the nation by Sir Hugh Lane (1875–1915). He started his career as an apprentice art restorer and later became a successful London art dealer. He drowned when the *Lusitania* sank in 1915. The collection includes work by Monet, Degas and Renoir, as well as by 20th-century Irish artists such as Yeats and Orpen, and modern European artists including Beuys and Albers.

www.hughlane.ie

✚ 132 F4 ✉ Charlemont House, Parnell Square North ☎ 874 1903 🕓 Tue–Thu 9.30–6, Fri–Sat 9.30–5, Sun 11–5 ✋ Free 🍴 Café (€) 🚉 Tara Street/Connolly 🚌 Cross-city buses ↔ Dublin Writers Museum (➤ 87) ❓ Guided tours by prior arrangement

a walk in the footsteps of Joyce

From the James Joyce Centre (► 30–31) in North Great George's Street walk down the street and cross over Parnell Street into Marlborough Street. Go past St Mary's Pro-Cathedral on the right. Take the second right into Earl Street North, where you will find a statue of Joyce. Turn left into O'Connell Street. Cross over, and as you pass the General Post Office (► 26–27) take the second right into Middle Abbey Street.

Outside Eason's bookshop (No 78–79) you will find the first of 14 bronze plaques in the pavement, marking the route taken by Leopold Bloom, hero of Joyce's novel *Ulysses*. Take time to read the quotes on the plaques.

Retrace your steps to O'Connell Street and turn right; there's another plaque outside No 49. Continue over the bridge.

On the corner of Aston Quay and Westmoreland Street is the Royal Liverpool Assurance building, with a plaque outside.

Cross over Westmoreland Street. On the left at No 29, formerly Harrison's bakery, is another plaque. Continue until you come to the traffic island with a statue of Thomas More and a further plaque. Continue with Trinity College to your left, up Grafton Street and take the third left into Duke Street.

On the right is Davy Byrne's pub, a haunt of both Joyce and his fictional hero Bloom.

Continue and turn right at the end into Dawson Street, taking the next left into Molesworth Street. Look for a plaque on the left. Cross into Kildare Street and the final plaque is across the road outside the old entrance to the National Museum (➤ 36–37).

Distance 2km (1.2 miles)
Time 1.5 hours, more including stops
Start point James Joyce Centre, 35 North Great George's Street
✚ 133 F5
End point National Museum, Kildare Street ✚ 136 D3
Lunch National Museum café, Kildare Street (€) ☎ 677 7444

JAMES JOYCE CENTRE

See pages 30–31.

NATIONAL BOTANIC GARDENS

To the north of the city, near Glasnevin Cemetery, are these botanic gardens, which opened in 1795. Apart from being a delightful place to stroll, they are also Ireland's premier centre for horticulture and botany. The heart of the gardens are the beautifully restored Victorian glass and cast-iron curvilinear buildings, including the Palm House. These glasshouses contain plants from across the world, including bamboo, banana and orchids. Outside, there is a rare handkerchief tree from China. In the Aquatic House you will find a

variety of Amazonian water lilies. The 20ha (50-acre) park has around 20,000 different species of flora. Particular highlights include an arboretum, rock garden, rose gardens, yew tree walk, the glorious herbaceous borders and a rare example of Victorian carpet bedding. An education and visitor centre opened in 2000 to give people further insight into the work of the botanic gardens.

➕ 132 A1 ✉ Glasnevin ☎ 857 0909 🕓 Summer, Mon–Sat 9–6, Sun 10–6; winter, daily 10–4.30. Glasshouses and Alpine House restricted hours ✋ Free 🚌 13, 19, 19A, 83 🚆 Drumcondra ◆ Glasnevin Cemetery (▶ 90–91) ❓ Guided tours available by prior arrangement (inexpensive)

NATIONAL WAX MUSEUM

At Dublin's Wax Museum you can have fun as you gain a little more insight into the historical characters that have helped to shape Ireland's history. In the Hall of Megastars you will find popular international entertainers, from Madonna and Elvis to Michael Jackson, and stars from the Irish music scene, including U2. You can learn more about Leonardo da Vinci through the impressive life-size replica of his painting, *The Last Supper*. The museum is due to move to Grafton Street in 2007.

➕ 135 B6 ✉ Smithfield Square, Smithfield ☎ 872 6340 for further information

O'CONNELL STREET

O'Connell Street became Dublin's main thoroughfare in 1794 when O'Connell Bridge was built. It is one of the busiest crossings over the River Liffey. Highlights on the street include the General Post Office (▶ 26–27) and Dublin's famous department store, Clery's. A statue of Daniel O'Connell overlooks the bridge. You can still see bullet marks from the fighting in 1916. O'Connell Street is currently undergoing a much needed face-lift and one of its newest attractions is The Spire (also known as the Monument of Light, ▶ 99), erected in 2002.

➕ 136 A2 ✉ O'Connell Street 🚆 Tara Street 🚌 Cross-city buses

OLD JAMESON DISTILLERY

This former distillery is in Smithfield Village (➤ 99), at the centre of the development of a once run-down area. The guided tour traces the history of Irish whiskey with exhibits and an audiovisual presentation. Whiskey was produced here from 1780 until 1971; it is now made in Middleton, Co Cork. Learn everything there is to know about Irish whiskey and how it differs from Scotch whisky, and don't miss the free dram in the Jameson Bar at the end of the tour. There is a huge choice of whiskey products for sale in the distillery shop.

www.whiskeytours.ie

✚ 135 B7 ✉ Bow Street, Smithfield ☎ 807 2355 🕐 Daily 9.30–6 (last tour at 5.30) 💷 Expensive 🍽 Restaurant, bar (€–€€) 🚊 Smithfield LUAS 🚌 68, 69, 79, 83, 90 ❓ Gift shop

PARNELL SQUARE

Laid out in 1755, this is the city's oldest Georgian square after St Stephen's Green (➤ 78). Today it is a shadow of its former glory, but it has many points of interest, including the Gate Theatre (➤ 90) and the Garden of Remembrance (open during daylight). This peaceful garden is dedicated to those who gave their lives for Irish independence. The focal point is the bronze *Children of Lír* sculpture by Oisín Kelly. Other highlights are the Dublin Writers Museum (➤ 87), the Hugh Lane Gallery (➤ 91) and the 1758 Rotunda Hospital, the oldest maternity hospital in the world.

✚ 132 F4 ✉ Parnell Square 🚊 Tara Street/Connolly 🚌 Cross-city buses

PHOENIX PARK

Phoenix Park is one of the largest city parks in Europe, if not the world, covering some 696ha (1,720 acres), and is encircled by a 13km (8-mile) wall. It was created in 1663 by King Charles II to provide a deer park. In 1745 it opened to the public and has been popular ever since. Ireland's tallest monument (63m/206ft), commemorating the Duke of Wellington's victory at Waterloo in 1815, can be found here. There's a lively historical interpretation of the park at the visitor centre and a children's exhibition on forest wildlife.

Adjoining the centre is Ashtown Castle, a medieval tower house with a miniature maze. On the northern side of the park is Áras an Uachtaráin, the official residence of the President of Ireland, built in the Palladian style in 1751 (guided tours every Saturday). The rest of the park, with its woodland, lakes and gardens, is a great place to stroll and watch the world go by.

✚ 130 E1 🚆 Heuston LUAS 🚌 10A, 25, 25A, 26, 66, 66A, 66B

Phoenix Park Visitor Centre

✉ Phoenix Park ☎ 677 0095 🕙 Park open daylight hours. Visitor centre: Apr–Sep daily 10–6; mid- to end Mar 10–5.30; Oct 10–5; Nov to mid-Mar Sat–Sun 10–5 💶 Park free; visitor centre moderate 🍴 Restaurant and café (€€–€) ❓ Free tickets for tours of Áras an Uachtaráin available at visitor centre

ST ANNE'S PARK

St Anne's Park was once the home of the Guinness family. The grounds were acquired by Dublin Corporation in 1939, and the house was finally demolished in 1968. The park consists of extensive woodlands, hidden walled gardens, a mile-long avenue of stately oaks that originally led up to the house, and the famous rose garden. This glorious park is best viewed between June and September. There are also many sporting facilities, including football pitches, tennis courts and a 12-hole golf course.

➕ 138 D8 (off map) ✉ Clontarf/Raheny ⏰ Summer, daily 9–7; winter, 10–dusk ✋ Free 🚉 Killester 🚌 130

ST MICHAN'S CHURCH

This church hides a grim secret in its crypt. The dry atmosphere caused bodies to mummify rather than decompose and, although the old coffins deteriorated and split open over time, the bodies remained intact, complete with hair and skin. A guided tour will show you this gruesome sight, with stories of those buried here, including the leaders of the 1798 rebellion, and barristers John and Henry Sheares. You can also see Wolfe Tone's death mask. The origins of the church can be traced back to 1095, although the current building was constructed in 1686. Inside highlights include

an organ believed to have been played by Handel and attractive woodcarvings of fruits and musical instruments above the choir.

🕂 135 B7 ✉ Church Street ☎ 872 4154
🕓 Mar–Oct Mon–Fri 10–12.30, 2–4.30, Sat 10–12.45; Nov–Feb Mon–Fri 12.30–2.30
✋ Moderate 🚇 Smithfield LUAS 🚌 83
❓ Access to vaults by tour only

SMITHFIELD

It's still all happening at Smithfield, the once run-down corner of the city.
Redevelopment of the old cattle market began in the early 1990s and continues. Central to the 'village' is the Old Jameson Distillery (➤ 96), no longer in production but running tours and selling whiskey-related merchandise. Towering over the whole area is the 56m-high (184ft) Chimney, built in 1895. You can take a ride to the top for panoramic views over Dublin. Duck Lane, with its restaurant and interior design shops, opens onto a new cobbled plaza featuring floodlights and overhead gas heaters.

🕂 135 A7 ✉ Smithfield Village ✋ Expensive 🚇 Smithfield LUAS 🚌 83

THE SPIRE

The Spire, also known as the Monument of Light, stands across the road from the General Post Office on the site where Nelson's Column used to be. Made of light reflective stainless steel, it is 120m (394ft) high, 3m (10ft) in diameter at the base and only 15cm (6in) at the top. It rises majestically above the rooftops where it sways gently (but safely) in the breeze. It is central to the rejuvenation of this somewhat down-at-heel area.

🕂 136 A2 ✉ O'Connell Street 🚇 Tara Street 🚌 Cross-city buses
↔ General Post Office (➤ 26–27)

Excursions

Avoca Handweavers	103
Bective Abbey	103
Booterstown Bird Sanctuary	104
Bray	104–105
Brú na Bóinne	106–107
Castletown House	108
Dalkey	108
Dollymount Strand	110
Drogheda	110–111
Dun Laoghaire and the National Maritime Museum	112
Glendalough	112–113
Hill of Tara	114–115
Howth	115
Kells	116
Kildare	116–117
Killiney	118
Malahide	118–119
Monasterboice	119
Powerscourt House and Gardens	120–121
Sandycove and James Joyce Tower	121
Slane	122
Trim	122–123
Wicklow Mountains National Park	124

From fine country houses and gardens to prehistoric tombs, from mountains, lakes and valleys to splendid golf courses – there is something for everyone in the eastern counties around Dublin. The pace of life is slower than in the city and you will need a car to visit the more remote areas, but many of the main attractions can be reached by public transport. To the southwest are the rolling green fields of Co Kildare, an area famous for horse breeding and its racecourse, the Curragh. South are the wild peaks of the Wicklow Mountains, where there are great opportunities for walking and touring. To the north the extraordinary ancient burial sites at Brú Na Bóinne dominate Co Meath and further north in Co Louth is the site of the famous Battle of the Boyne of 1690.

AVOCA HANDWEAVERS

Located in the heart of Co Wicklow, in the village of Avoca, the handweavers began spinning and weaving blankets and clothing in 1723. The business, however, did not really flourish until the 1920s, when the Wynne sisters inherited the mill and with flair and ingenuity built an excellent venture marketing tweeds all over the world, supplying top-class designers and selling to royalty. It expanded with the introduction of rugs and throws using natural fibres, including lambswool and cashmere in a brilliant range of colours. You can visit the mill to see production in progress and hopefully pick up a bargain in the factory shop. The village has another claim to fame – it was the location for the popular BBC television drama *Ballykissangel*.
www.avoca.ie

✚ 138 E3 ✉ Old Mill, Avoca, Co Wicklow ☎ 0402 35105 🕐 Daily 9–6 (9.30–5.30 in winter) ✋ Free 🚌 Bus Éireann 133 to Avoca (service infrequent)

BECTIVE ABBEY

The original abbey was built in 1147 by Murchad, King of Meath. Little of the early building survives and what you can see in a field

by the River Boyne is really the ruin of a 15th-century fortified building – more castle than monastery. The abbey was repressed in 1536 and fell into disrepair. What remains gives an indication of a religious, defensive and domestic building. The religious aspects are the cloisters – the best-preserved part of the building – the nave and the chapter house. The defensive parts can be seen in the square tower and the domestic parts in the remains of fireplaces, chimneys and windows.

✚ 138 B2 ✉ Bective, Navan, Co Meath ☎ 046 943 7227 🕐 Daily, daylight hours ✋ Free 🚌 Bus Éireann service 109 Dublin to Navan, then 135 Navan to Scurloughstown stops at Bective Cross

BOOTERSTOWN BIRD SANCTUARY

Booterstown Marsh is the only bird sanctuary in South Dublin Bay, an important feeding and roosting area for ducks, geese and waders. As part of the bay, Booterstown Marsh is an essential stop-over and refuelling place for migrating birds. There are both freshwater and saltwater habitats and the birds include moorhen, teal, snipe, oystercatchers and Brent geese. During the 19th century most of the marsh was used for cultivation or grazing but was drained and subsequently used for gardens. After World War II, when it fell into disuse, the marsh vegetation gradually reclaimed the arable land and now it is administered by the National Trust for Ireland; further development should include an interpretation centre and hide (concealed shelter).

✚ 138 D3 ✉ Booterstown, Co Dublin ☎ The National Trust for Ireland 454 1786 🕐 Dawn–dusk 🚉 Booterstown

BRAY

This former refined Victorian seaside resort has become a playground for families and day-trippers. The safe sand and shingle beach stretches for 1.5km (1 mile) and can get very crowded in summer. You might prefer to walk along the cliffs at Bray Head, which, at 241m (790ft) above the sea, offer great views. On the seafront is the fascinating conservation-conscious National Sea Life Centre. Other activities in Bray include golf, sailing and fishing. Alternatively you can just wander along the esplanade that stretches from Bray Harbour to Bray Head and watch the world go by.

Just outside the town, at the foot of the Little Sugar Loaf mountain, is beautiful **Kilruddery House and Gardens.** The house was originally built in the 17th century, but was remodelled in Elizabethan style in the 1820s. There are carvings by Grinling Gibbons and furniture by Chippendale, and a lovely orangery, added in 1852, has some remarkable marble statues. The superb gardens, the oldest formal gardens in Ireland, were created in the 1680s in the French style.

✚ 138 D3 🚆 Bray 🚌 45, 84

🛈 Old Courthouse, Main Street Bray, Co Wicklow ☎ 286 7128

Kilruddery House and Gardens

✉ Bray ☎ 286 3405; www.kilruddery.com 🕐 Gardens: Apr–Sep daily 1–5; house: May, Jun, Sep daily 1–5 ✋ House and garden: expensive; garden only: moderate 🚆 Bray, then Finnegan bus stops close to entrance 🚌 84 from Dublin stops at Woodlands Hotel, then short walk to entrance

BRÚ NA BÓINNE

The Boyne Valley is strewn with some of Ireland's most important archaeological monuments. Brú Na Bóinne (Palace of the Boyne) has Europe's richest concentration of ancient monuments, including forts, henges, standing stones and the mysterious grand passage tombs of Newgrange, Knowth and Dowth. To understand the significance of the site you need to realize that these monuments are 1,000 years older than England's Stonehenge and 100 years older than the pyramids of Giza in Egypt. The River Boyne valley was first settled during the Stone Age and it is possible the pre-Celtic founders may have come from the Iberian Peninsula, but many other legends surround the site. Take a look around the visitor centre for background information before embarking on a tour. In high summer you should book well in advance as the tours are restricted to 700 visitors a day.

Newgrange

Newgrange was probably built more than 5,000 years ago by skilled builders. This is evident from the excellent condition of the tombs. The spectacular passage grave here is the high point of a visit. Built into a giant mound 85m (280ft) across and 10m (33ft) high, its perimeter is defined by nearly a hundred massive kerbstones (curbstones). The exterior is faced with brilliant white quartzite. At least 200,000 tons of stone went into its construction, with stones as large as 16 tons each brought from as far away as Co Wicklow. At the entrance to the tomb one of these kerbstones is marked with the distinctive spiral details of this area and above it is a rectangular opening like a mail box. It is through this roof box that the dawn light enters at the winter solstice and shines through to the interior. A lottery system gives people the chance to witness this event, otherwise you will have to make do with with a simulated experience. A guide leads you by torchlight along the 19m-long (62ft) passage into the heart of the mound and to the burial chamber, with its intricate corbelled ceiling rising

6m (20ft) above you. Here is the most amazing spiral abstract carved detail in the walls. When the tomb was excavated only a few bodies were found, unusual considering the tomb's size. It is possible that remains were removed regularly.

Knowth

You can see the great tomb of Knowth from the road, but you can access it only by taking a tour. This mound is defined by some 120

kerbstones and is surrounded by at least 17 small passage graves. Inside the main tomb (closed to visitors) are two passages and the stonework is rich with spiral and line carvings. The exterior is also beautifully decorated.

Dowth

Dowth contains some of the finest rock carvings anywhere in Ireland. It can be viewed from the road to the east of Newgrange. The passage grave here was heavily excavated by the Victorians and became popular with souvenir hunters.

🕂 138 B2 ✉ Donore, Co Meath ☎ 041 988 0300/0305 🕙 Mar–Apr daily 9.30–5.30; May daily 9–6.30; Jun to mid-Sep daily 9–7; mid-Sep to end Sep daily 9–6.30; Oct daily 9.30–5; Nov–Feb daily 9.30–5. Knowth open: May–Oct only 👋 Varies according to site; visitor centre only: inexpensive 🍴 Tea room at visitor centre (€) 🚌 Bus Éireann 100 Dublin to Drogheda, then 163 to Donore village (10-min walk)

❓ Access to monuments by tour only, lasting 1 hour 15 mins (allow at least 3 hours if visiting both Newgrange and Knowth). Last tour departs 1 hour 45 mins before centre closes but it's best to visit early as it is often overcrowded and visitors are regularly turned away

CASTLETOWN HOUSE

This striking house was built in the Palladian style between 1722 and 1732 for the Speaker of the Irish Parliament and at the time Ireland's richest man, William Connolly. From humble beginnings, Connolly amassed his wealth by buying and selling forfeited property in the aftermath of the Battle of the Boyne in 1690. Castletown's opulent interior has elaborate rococo stucco work and a Long Gallery decorated in the Pompeian style of the 1770s. Look for the huge painting called *The Boar Hunt* by Paul de Vos (1569–1679) in the main hall. Connolly did not see the project through and died before the house was completed; his widow continued improvements. Her main contribution was Connolly's Folly, an unusual obelisk structure some 40m (130ft) high, 3km (2 miles) north of the house. The magnificent interiors of the house were subsequently completed by Lady Louisa Connolly, wife of William Connolly's great nephew, who moved here in 1759. One fascinating room is the Print Room, lined with elaborately framed prints from 18th-century magazines.

✚ 138 C2 ✉ Celbridge, Co Kildare ☎ 628 8252 🕐 Easter Sun–Sep Mon–Fri 10–6, Sat, Sun and public hols 1–6; Oct Mon–Fri 10–5, Sun and public hols 1–5 ✋ Moderate 🍴 Coffee shop (€) 🚌 67, 67A, 67N, 67X
❓ Guided tour only, lasts approximately 1 hour

DALKEY

South of the city is the pretty seaside village of Dalkey, once called the 'town of seven castles'. Only two of these fortified houses now remain, standing opposite each other in the main street. Goat Castle remains totally intact and houses the **Heritage Centre,** with displays on the once important port. The view of the sea and mountains from the battlements is splendid. In summer you can visit Dalkey Island by boat, just a short distance offshore.

Dalkey Castle and Heritage Centre

✚ 138 D3 ✉ Castle Street, Dalkey ☎ 285 8366; www.dalkeycastle.com
🕐 Mon–Fri 9.30–5, Sat–Sun and public hols 11–5 ✋ Moderate 🚇 Dalkey

DOLLYMOUNT STRAND

Only 20 minutes from the city centre, Dollymount Strand is a 3km (2-mile) beach, a perfect place for walking, paddling or flying a kite. Nearby North Bull Island, a 300ha (741-acre) island formed after the construction of the Bull Wall (a North Sea wall) in the 1820s, is an important nature reserve and bird sanctuary with some 25,000 wading birds visiting in winter. You can drive on to the expanse of sand via a bridge at the west end and a causeway in the middle. A visitor centre opens in summer (daily 10–4.30) to help with the identification of wildlife. There are splendid views across the bay to the Wicklow Mountains. ✚ 138 C3 ✉ North Bull Island, Causeway Road, off James Larking Road ✋ Free 🚋 Clontarf Road 20 mins 🚌 130

DROGHEDA

The town of Drogheda stands at the lowest bridging point of the River Boyne, just a few kilometres from the site of the famous Battle of the Boyne in 1690. It was first established by Viking traders in 911 and was an important Norman port in the 14th century. Little remains of the town walls but there are still elements of medieval architecture in the hilly streets, including St Lawrence's Gate, a fine four-floor barbican (tower). Also of interest is the Magdalene Tower, the only remains of the original Dominican friary of 1224. Above the south bank of the river – accessed from the riverside by steep steps – is the Norman motte (castle mound), topped by a Martello tower (c1808), with splendid views over the town. It is also the site of the **Millmount Museum,** housed in the old barracks, with exhibits relating to the town and its industries, an authentic 19th-century kitchen and a craft centre showcasing Irish design, including jewellery, knitwear and ceramics.

✚ 138 B3 🚌 Bus Éireann service 163 to Drogheda 🚉 Drogheda ℹ️ Tourist Information ✉️ Bus Éireann Depot, Donore Road, Drogheda, Co Louth ☎️ 041 983 7070

Millmount Museum

✉️ Millmount Square, Drogheda, Co Louth ☎️ 041 983 3097 🕐 Mon–Sat 10–6, Sun and public hols 2.30–6 ✋ Moderate

DUN LAOGHAIRE AND THE NATIONAL MARITIME MUSEUM

Dun Laoghaire (pronounced 'Dun Leary') has a fine harbour and is well known both as a seaside resort and a thriving port where car ferries from Holyhead on the Isle of Anglesey in Wales dock. From a small fishing village in the early 19th century, the town is now a thriving community and a popular place for the people of Dublin to visit on weekends. There's plenty to do, with lots of pubs and restaurants, water sports, boat trips around the bay and fishing, plus excellent walking and views along the coast. The **National Maritime Museum** in the Mariner's Church has displays of model boats and Irish naval memorabilia. Take a look at the Bantry boat, a 12m (40ft) French longboat captured during the failed French invasion of 1796; it remains in excellent condition.

➕ 138 D3 🚇 Dun Laoghaire 🚌 7, 7A, 46A, 746

National Maritime Museum

✉ High Terrace, Dun Laoghaire ☎ 280 0969 🕐 May–Sep Tue–Sun 1–5 ✋ Free (donations welcome)

GLENDALOUGH

Deep in the heart of the Wicklow Mountains are the atmospheric remains of a remarkable monastic settlement founded in the 6th century by St Kevin, who came from one of Leinster's ruling families. He was abbot of Glendalough until his death in AD618 and the monastery became famous throughout Europe as a seat of learning. It remained an important place of pilgrimage well into the 18th century. The site is one of Ireland's premier attractions and can get very busy in high summer; the best time to visit is a quiet spring or autumn evening. The setting is magnificent, with the lake and the mountains making a superb backdrop, and the area is particularly popular with walkers. The ruins incorporate a 12th-century round tower and 11th-century St Kevin's Church, known as St Kevin's Kitchen. The roofless cathedral of St Peter and St Paul dates from the 12th century and is the largest ruin. There are several other churches and monastic buildings around the site, as well as numerous gravestones and crosses. Some of the remains, although visible from the shore, are accessible only by boat, including the Tempull na Skellig or 'church on the rock' and St Kevin's Bed, a small cave reputed to have been the saint's retreat. The visitor centre, also the information centre for the Wicklow Mountains National Park (➤ 124), has an audiovisual presentation to the site, and its interactive displays give a good insight into the life and times of St Kevin and the monastery.

🚌 Glendalough bus twice daily from Bray and Dublin

Visitor Centre

✚ 138 E3 ✉ Glendalough, Bray, Co Wicklow ☎ 0404 45325/45352
🕐 Daily 9.30–5 (Mar–Oct 9.30–6) ✋ Inexpensive ❓ Guided tour on request, 30–40 mins

HILL OF TARA

At first sight it may seem as if you are looking at a few grassy
humps and depressions in the landscape, but it is worth the trip,
not just for the superb views, but for the sense of history and
mythology evoked by this important neolithic place. Tara was
the main religious and political centre of Ireland during the
first millennium AD, where priests and kings would gather. It
remained the seat of the High Kings until the 6th century;
although its connection to royalty remained until the 11th century,
its importance was waning by this time with the spread of
Christianity. Among the more impressive remains is the Mound
of Hostages, a passage grave that, on excavation, revealed 40
Bronze Age cremations from around 2000BC. One of the most
prominent earthworks is the Royal Enclosure with a ring fort
known as Cormac's House in the centre. Here stands a pillar,
called Lia Faíl, or Stone of Destiny, where the High Kings

of Ireland were crowned. There is a visitor centre on site in
St Patrick's Church, with an audiovisual display and tours of
the site.

✚ 138 C2 ✉ Near Navan, Co Meath ☎ 046 90 25903 🕓 Main site open
during daylight hours. Visitor centre in St Patrick's Church mid-May to mid-Sep
daily 10–6 ✋ Inexpensive 🍴 Café near site (€) 🚌 Bus Éireann service 109
to Tara Cross (ask driver for stop) ❓ Guided tours, 40 mins

HOWTH

A pleasant ride north on the DART will take you to Howth, a major
fishing centre and yachting harbour. Howth (rhymes with both) is
a popular residential suburb whose steep streets run down to the
sea. The DART station is near the harbour and close to all the
waterside activity, bars, pubs and restaurants. You can take a boat
trip to view the small rocky island, Ireland's Eye, with its resident
puffin colony, Martello tower and 6th-century monastic ruins.
Above the town are the remains of St Mary's Abbey and 1km
(0.5 miles) to the west is Howth Castle and the **National
Transport Museum.** The 16th-century castle is closed to the
public but the gardens are famous for their rhododendrons and
azaleas. Hidden away in a farmyard is the transport museum, with
its unique collection of restored old trams, fire engines and vans.
From Howth Head there are splendid views over Dublin Bay, and

an 8km (5-mile) path around the
head makes a dramatic walk.

✚ 138 C3 ✉ Howth Head 🚉 Howth
🚌 31, 31B

National Transport Museum

✉ Heritage Depot, Howth Castle
Demesne, Howth ☎ 848 0831;
www.nationaltransportmuseum.org
🕓 Jun–Aug daily 10–5; Sep–May
Sat–Sun and public hols 2–5
✋ Inexpensive

KELLS (CEANANNUS MOR)

You probably wouldn't visit the town of Kells if it wasn't for its connection with the famous book, and a visit to the heritage centre puts the Book of Kells and the monastery into historical context. A monastery was founded here in AD550, but it was not until the early 9th century that the monks came with their famous illuminated manuscript from Iona, fleeing the Viking raids. The work was completed in Kells and displays in the heritage centre allow you to view the pages on computer. The book is now in Dublin's Trinity College Library (➤ 40–41), but there are some good replicas here to view.

✚ 138 B2 🚌 Bus Éireann service 109 to Kells

Kells Heritage Centre

✉ The Courthouse, Headfort Place, Kells, Co Meath ☎ 046 92 47840
🕐 May–Sep Mon–Sat 10–5.30, Sun and public hols 1.30–6; Oct–Apr Tue–Sat 10–5 ✋ Moderate 🍴 Café (€)

KILDARE

Since Kildare got its bypass in 2003, the centre has become pleasantly quiet. In the old Market House is the tourist information office, and a heritage centre that traces the history of Kildare and its surroundings. The town is dominated by St Brigid's Cathedral, built on the site of a former 5th-century monastery. The original 10th-century tower survives and is an impressive 33m (108ft) high.

Co Kildare is horseracing country and the home of the famous racecourse, the Curragh. Just south of Kildare is Tully House and the **Irish National Stud,** which was founded in 1900 by Colonel William Hall-Walker; now a state-run stud, it breeds some of the most famous racehorses in the world. The best time to visit the stables is between February and July, when there can be as many as 300 foals. Tours of the stable blocks and paddocks are available and there is a Horse Museum illustrating the importance of horses and racing to the Irish. Look out for the skeleton of Arkle, one of the stud's most famous champion stallions.

The **Japanese Gardens** at Tully House, landscaped between 1906 and 1910, include an impressive array of plants, from mulberry and cherry trees to magnolias and bamboo. There is a tea house and a miniature village carved out of rock from Mount Fuji.

The garden symbolizes the journey of a soul from Birth to Eternity, finally coming to rest in the Garden of Peace and Contentment. Along the way the soul encounters the Hill of Learning, the Walk of Wisdom, the Hill of Ambition and the Bridge of Life.

Also at Tully House is **St Fiachra's Garden,** a millennium project that seeks to re-create a monastic island hermitage in honour of St Fiachra, the patron saint of gardeners. Its use of natural materials, such as rock and water, creates a sense of spirituality and calm. You can see a stone cave decorated in sparkling Waterford Crystal and the statue of St Fiachra holding a seed standing on a rock in the lake.

✚ 138 D1 🚌 Bus Éireann service 126 to Kildare 🚉 Kildare
🛈 Tourist Information ✉ Market House, Market Square, Co Kildare
☎ 045 521240 🕐 Mon–Fri 10–1, 2–5

Irish National Stud/Japanese Gardens/St Fiachra's Garden

✉ Tully, Kildare ☎ 045 521617 🕐 Mid-Feb to mid-Nov daily 9.30–6
✋ Expensive (covers both gardens and National Stud) 🍴 Restaurant (€€)
🚌 Bus Éireann service 126 to Kildare, stops at gate 🚉 Kildare ❓ Guided tour of the National Stud, allow one hour

KILLINEY

A short trip south on the DART takes you to Killiney, the 'Dublin Riviera', where national and international celebrities have set up home. But you don't have to be wealthy to enjoy some of the best views of Dublin and the surrounding area. The climb to the top of Killiney Hill takes about 30 minutes and rewards with exceptional vistas. Down at Coliemore Harbour fishermen run boat trips in summer to nearby Dalkey Island, with its bird sanctuary.

✚ 138 D3 ✉ Killiney 🚊 Killiney

MALAHIDE

Just 13km (8 miles) north of Dublin, and easily reached by the DART, is Malahide. This attractive seaside village has become an increasingly desirable place for Dubliners to live, and its pubs, restaurants, chic shops and marina make it popular with visitors too. One of the highlights on the edge of the village is **Malahide Castle.** Set in 100ha (247 acres) of woodland, the castle was both a fortress and a private home for nearly 800 years; the Talbot family lived here continuously from 1188 until 1973.

It is an interesting mix of architectural styles, with its central medieval core, a three-level, 12th-century tower, 16th-century oak room and additional Georgian embellishments and furnishings. On organized tours you can see the Talbot family portraits, together with paintings loaned by the National Gallery. Keep an eye out for one of the many ghosts believed to haunt the castle. In a separate building on the grounds you will find the Fry Model Railway.

✚ 138 C3 🚉 Malahide 🚌 42

Malahide Castle

✉ Malahide Castle Demense, Malahide ☎ 846 2184
🕐 Apr–Sep Mon–Sat 10–5, Sun and public hols 11–6;
Oct–Mar Mon–Sat 10–5, Sun and public hols 11–5
👋 Expensive 🍴 Restaurant (€€)

MONASTERBOICE

The ruins of the monastery of St Buite, one of the most famous monastic settlements in Ireland, lie in a secluded spot north of Drogheda. Founded in the 6th century, the monastery remained at the height of importance for 600 years until it was superseded by the new Cistercian foundation, Mellifont Abbey. Highlights are the 10th-century roofless round tower and the three high crosses. The finest is Muiredach's Cross, with sculptural detail and an inscription that reads 'A prayer for Muiredach by whom was made this cross'.

✚ 138 B3 ✉ Near Drogheda, Co Louth 🕐 Always accessible 👋 Free 🚌 Bus Éireann 100 to Monasterboice Inn

POWERSCOURT HOUSE AND GARDENS

Set amid the wild landscape of the Wicklow Mountains, Powerscourt is one of the most magnificent gardens, both formal and semi-natural, in Europe. The view from the terrace is unbeatable, with its sweeping vista and a backdrop of mountain peaks. The original house, built in the 1740s, was gutted by fire in 1974 and has been the subject of a careful restoration project. It now houses an exhibition on the history of Powerscourt. You can visit the former ballroom, and there is a gallery of craft and design shops and a terrace restaurant. But it is for the gardens that most visitors come; laid out in the mid-18th century, they comprise great formal terraces that drop down towards lakes and fountains, statues and decorative ironwork. There are American, Japanese and Italian gardens, as well as charming walled gardens with rose beds and borders, and even a pets' cemetery. The leaflet provided

will give you a self-guided tour of the gardens, or you can take a formal tour. If time allows, check out the 121m-high (397ft) waterfall, Ireland's highest, 5km (3 miles) away but on the Powerscourt Estate.

www.powerscourt.ie

✚ 138 D3 ✉ Powerscourt Estate, Enniskerry, Co Wicklow ☎ 204 6000 🕐 Daily 9.30–5.30. Waterfall: summer until 7pm; winter open from 10.30–dusk ✋ Expensive for house and gardens, free to enter estate 🍴 Restaurant and café (€–€€) 🚌 44 🚊 Bray, then 185 bus ❓ Guided tour lasts 40 mins. Garden centre on site

SANDYCOVE AND JAMES JOYCE TOWER

Just south of Dun Laoghaire is the affluent village and popular commuter suburb of Sandycove. It is named after a small sandy cove near the rocky point on which a Martello tower was built in 1804 to withstand a threatened invasion along this coastline by Napoleon. James Joyce stayed in the tower for a week and it features in the opening chapter of his famous novel *Ulysses*. It now houses a small museum of Joycean memorabilia, including a collection of letters, photographs, first and rare editions and personal possessions of the author, including his guitar and walking stick. If you fancy a swim, directly below the tower is the Forty Foot Pool (complete with changing areas), traditionally an all-male nude bathing pool, but now open to both sexes; swimming costumes permitted!

James Joyce Museum

✚ 138 D3 ✉ James Joyce Tower, Sandycove ☎ 280 9265 🕐 Mar–Oct Mon–Sat 10–1, 2–5, Sun and public hols 2–6 ✋ Moderate 🚊 Sandycove 🚌 59 from Dun Laoghaire

SLANE

Despite suffering from
heavy traffic congestion,
the estate village of Slane
is a pleasant place to visit,
with its fine Georgian
houses. To escape from the busy main street head up the winding
lane to the Hill of Slane. From this spot, St Patrick is said to have lit
a fire announcing the arrival of Christianity and heralding the end
of the pagan Kings of Tara. Here are the remains of a church and
college established in 1512. **Slane Castle,** to the west of the
village, has been home to the Conynham family since the 18th
century. The castle suffered a devastating fire in 1991 and after ten
years of renovation reopened to the public in 2001. You can see the
fine Gothic Ballroom with its beautiful plasterwork ceiling
completed for the visit of George IV in 1821. The grounds of the
castle were landscaped by Capability Brown. Now mostly used for
conferences, weddings and concerts, Slane Castle has also served
as a location for several films and U2 recorded their album, The
Unforgettable Fire, here in 1984.

Slane Castle

✚ 138 B2 ✉ Slane, Co Meath ☎ 041 988 4400; www.slanecastle.ie 🕐 2
May–2 Aug Sun–Thu 12–5 👆 Expensive 🚌 Bus Éireann service 177 to Slane

TRIM

Trim is a thriving town on the River Boyne, and was once the site
of one of the oldest and largest religious settlements in Ireland.
The town is dominated by the Anglo-Norman **Trim Castle,** which
was built by Hugh de Lacy in 1173. It is the largest such castle in
Ireland, enclosing a 1.2ha (3-acre) site. The castle has hardly been
altered since the 13th century and still bears the scars of warfare.
Visitors can access the 21m-high (69ft) keep and grounds on a
guided tour. Scenes from the 1995 epic film Braveheart were shot
here. Across the Boyne are the ruins of Sheep's Gate and the

Yellow Steeple – the belfry tower of the former St Mary's Augustinian Abbey dating from 1368 and the most prominent remains here. It rises dramatically from the quiet meadow, left undisturbed since the town developed on the opposite bank in the 18th century. Other ruins of note are the 13th-century Cathedral of St Peter and St Paul and the Hospital of John the Baptist. The visitor centre gives more insight into these medieval ruins in its exhibition, The Power and the Glory, a clever multimedia display that underlines the consequences of the Norman arrival in Ireland.

✚ 138 C2 🚌 Bus Éireann service 111 to Trim

Trim Visitor Centre

✉ Castle Street, Trim, Co Meath ☎ 046 94 37227 🕐 Mon–Sat 10–5, Sun and public hols 12–5.30. Closed Thu 12.30–1.30 ✋ Moderate

Trim Castle

✉ Trim, Co Meath ☎ 046 94 38619 🕐 Easter–Oct daily 10–6; Nov–Easter weekends 10–5 ✋ Inexpensive; moderate including keep tour ❓ Guided tours only to keep, 40 mins

WICKLOW MOUNTAINS NATIONAL PARK

A dramatic, secluded area of high mountains, peaceful valleys and lakes on the doorstep of Dublin, this park covers some 20,000ha (49,420 acres) with Lugnaquilla its highest point at 943m (3,094ft). Two scenic passes cross the mountains from east to west – the Sally Gap on the spectacular old military road from Dublin to Laragh, and the Wicklow Gap to the south. Much of the lower mountain slopes are covered in woodland; some trees are believed to be old enough to have supplied the timber for Dublin's St Patrick's Cathedral and London's Palace of Westminster. In the western foothills, several valleys have been flooded to form the Poulaphouca Reservoir, also known as Blessington Lake. This provides Dublin with water and electricity, and you can take a boat trip on the water. Scattered throughout the park are ancient hillforts and stone circles, as well as monastic sites such as Glendalough (➤ 112–113). Also within the park is Powerscourt House and Gardens (➤ 120–121).

✚ 138 E3 🚌 Glendalough bus twice daily from Dublin and Bray

Information Point

✉ Upper Lough, Glendalough, Wicklow Mountains National Park, Co Wicklow ☎ 0404 45425 🕐 May–Sep, daily 10–6; Oct–Apr, weekends 10–dusk ✋ Free

Index

Abbey Theatre 82
airports and air services 12, 14
Áras an Uachtaráin 97
The Ark 56
Ashtown Castle 97
Avoca Handweavers 103

Baggot Street Bridge 66
Ballsbridge 62
Ballykissangel 103
Bank of Ireland 62–63
Bank of Ireland Arts Centre 63
banks 17
Bective Abbey 103
Behan, Brendan 63, 91
Bewley's Oriental Cafés 63
Blessington Lake 124
Blessington Street Basin 82–83
Bloomsday 10, 31
Book of Kells 40–41
Booterstown Bird Sanctuary 104
Boyne Valley 106
Bram Stoker Dracula Experience 83
Bray 104–105
Brazen Head 58
breakdowns 13
breath-testing 13
Brú na Bóinne 106–107
buses 12, 13, 14

canals 66
car rental 15
The Casino, Marino 84
Castletown House 108
Chester Beatty Library 25
Children of Lír 96
The Chimney 99
Christ Church Cathedral 22–23, 58
City Hall 46–47, 59
climate and seasons 8
clothing sizes 19
Collins, Michael 85, 90
Collins Barracks 85

concessions 15
currency 18
Custom House 86–87

Dalkey 108
Dalkey Island 108
DART 13
De Valera, Eámon 32, 75, 90
dental services 9
Dollymount Strand 110
Dowth 107
Drimnagh Castle 47
drinking water 19
driving 8, 13
Drogheda 110–111
drugs and medicines 18
Dublin Castle 24–25
Dublin City Library and Archive 64
Dublin Writers Museum 87
Dublin Zoo 88–89
Dun Laoghaire 112
Dvblinia 48, 58

Easter Rising 26–27, 32, 73
electricity 17
embassies and consulates 16
emergency telephone numbers 17
excursions 100–124

ferry services 12
festivals and events 10–11
film festival 10
Fitzwilliam Square 64–65
Four Courts 89
Fusiliers' Arch 78

GAA Museum, Croke Park 89
Gallery of Photography 56
Gate Theatre 90, 96
genealogy 73
General Post Office 26–27
Georgian Dublin 71, 75
Glasnevin Cemetery 90–91

Glendalough 112–113
Grafton Street 65
Grand Canal 66
Guinness Storehouse 28–29

Ha'penny Bridge 48–49
health advice 8, 9, 18–19
Heraldic Museum 66–67
Hill of Tara 114–115
Hopkins, Gerard Manley 91
Horse Museum 116
Howth 115
Hugh Lane Gallery 91

insurance 8, 9
Ireland's Eye 115
Irish Jewish Museum 49
Irish Museum of Modern Art 50
Irish National Stud 116, 117
Iveagh House and Gardens 67

James Joyce Centre 30–31, 92
James Joyce Museum 121
James Joyce Tower 121
Japanese Gardens 117
jazz festival 10
Joyce, James 10, 30–31, 50, 75, 92–93, 121

Kavanagh, Patrick 63, 66
Kells (Ceanannus Mor) 116
Kildare 116–117
Killiney 118
Kilmainham Gaol 32–33
Kilruddery House and Gardens 105
Knowth 107

Leinster House 71
Liffey Swim 10
LUAS light rail 14
Lugnaquilla 124

Malahide 118–119
Marsh's Library 50
medical treatment 9

Meeting House Square 56
Merrion Square 71
Millmount Museum 111
Monasterboice 119
money 18
Muiredach's Cross 119
museum opening hours 17
music festivals 10–11

National Botanic Gardens
    94–95
National Gallery 34–35
national holidays 11
National Library 72–73
National Maritime Museum
    112
National Museum 36–37
National Museum of
    Decorative Arts and
    History 85
National Photographic
    Archive 56, 73
National Print Museum 73
National Transport Museum
    115
National Wax Museum 95,
    99
Natural History Museum 74
Newgrange 106–107
Newman House 75, 78
North Bull Island 110
Number Twenty Nine 71, 75

O'Connell, Daniel 50, 90
O'Connell Street 95
Oireachtas (parliament) 71
Old Jameson Distillery 96
opening hours 17
Oscar Wilde's House 76

Parnell, Charles Stewart
    90
Parnell Square 96
passports and visas 8

Pearse, Pádraic 26–27
personal safety 19
pharmacies 17, 18
Phoenix Park 97
photography 19
police 17, 19
Poulaphouca Reservoir
    124
Powerscourt House and
    Gardens 120–121
public transport 12–13, 14

Rotunda Hospital 96
Royal College of Surgeons
    76, 78

St Anne's Park 98
St Ann's Church 77
St Audoen's churches 52
St Fiachra's Garden 117
St Kevin 112
St Michan's Church 98–99
St Patrick 38, 122
St Patrick's Cathedral 38–39,
    58
St Patrick's Day 10
St Stephen's Green 78
St Valentine 57
St Werburgh's Church 58
Sally Gap 124
Sandycove 121
seat belts 13
senior citizens 15
Shaw, George Bernard 53
Shaw's Birthplace 53
Slane 122
Smithfield 99
speed limits 13
The Spire (Monument of
    Light) 99
Stoker, Bram 77, 83
student travellers 15
Sunlight Chambers 53
Swift, Jonathan 38–39

taxis 13, 14–15
telephones 16–17
Temple Bar 55–56
Temple Bar Gallery 56
tipping 18
Tone, Wolfe 77, 78, 98
tourist offices 9, 16
train services 13, 14
Trim 122–123
Trim Castle 122, 123
Trinity College 40–41

Ulysses 30–31
University Church 79

Viking and medieval Dublin
    58–59

walks
    Dublin's pubs 68–69
    Footsteps of Joyce 92–93
    Viking and medieval Dublin
    58–59
War Memorial Gardens
    56–57
Waterways Visitor Centre
    79
websites 9
whiskey 96
Whitefriar Street Carmelite
    Church 57
Wicklow Gap 124
Wicklow Mountains 124
Wicklow Mountains National
    Park 124
Wilde, Oscar 71, 76

Yeats, Jack B 35, 64
Yeats, W B 71, 82, 91
Yeats Museum 35

Acknowledgements

The Automobile Association would like to thank the following photographers, companies and picture libraries for their assistance in the preparation of this book.

Abbreviations for the picture credits are as follows – (t) top; (b) bottom; (c) centre; (l) left; (r) right; (AA) AA World Travel Library

4l St Patrick's Day Parade, AA/S Day; **4c** Trinity College, AA/S Day; **4r** O'Shea's Merchant Pub, AA/M Short; **5l** Malahide Castle, AA; **5c** Bective Abbey, AA/C Jones; **5r** Howth Head, AA/M Short; **6/7** St Patrick's Day Parade, AA/S Day; **10** St Patrick's Day Parade, AA/S Day; **11** Dublin Marathon, AA/S Whitehorne; **12** Sealink Ferry, AA/M Short; **13** Dart Train, AA/M Short; **14** General Post Office, AA/S Day; **15** South Great George's Street, AA/S Whitehorne; **16** Tourist Information Centre, AA/S Day; **18** Green Post Box, AA/S Whitehorne; **20/21** Trinity College, AA/S Day; **22** Christ Church Cathedral casket, AA/S Day; **22/23t** Christ Church Cathedral, AA; **22/23b** Christ Church Cathedral crypt, AA/S Day; **24/25t** Dublin Castle interior, AA/S Day; **24/25b** Dublin Castle exterior, AA/S Day; **25** Chester Beatty Library, AA; **26** General Post Office, AA/S Day; **26/27** Cuchuliann Statue, AA/S Day; **28/29** Guinness Storehouse, AA/S Day; **30** Joyce Centre, AA/S Day; **30/31** Joyce Centre, AA/S Day; **31** Joyce Centre, AA/S Day; **32** Kilmainham Gaol, AA/S McBride; **32/33** Kilmainham Jail, AA/S Whitehorne; **34/35** National Gallery, AA; **36** National Museum, AA/S Whitehorne; **36/37** National Museum, AA/S Day; **38** St Patrick's Cathedral, AA/S Whitehorne; **39t** St Patrick's Cathedral exterior AA/S Day; **39b** Jonathan Swift Death Mask, AA/S Day; **40** Trinity College, AA/L Blake; **40/41** Trinity College Library, AA/S McBride; **42/43** O'Shea's Merchant Pub, AA/M Short; **45** Sunlight Chambers, AA; **46/47** City Hall Dome, AA/S Day; **48/49** Ha'penny Bridge, AA/S Whitehorne; **50** Dublin Royal Hospital Museum, AA/M Short; **51** Marsh's Library, AA/S Day; **52** St Auden's Church, AA; **53** Shaw's Birthplace, AA/S Day; **54** Crown Alley, AA/S Day; **55** Temple Bar Square, AA/S Day; **56/57** Whitefriars Carmelite Church, AA/S Whitehorne; **59** St Audeon's Arch, AA/S Day; **60** St Patrick's Day AA/S Day; **61** St Stephen's Green, AA/S Day; **62/63** Bank of Ireland, AA; **64** Fitzwilliam Square, AA; **64/65** Grafton Street, AA/S Day; **66** Grand Canal, AA/S Whitehorne; **67** Dublin Heraldic Museum, AA/S Day; **69** Stag's Head Pub, AA/S McBride; **70** Merrion Square North, AA/M Short; **71** Leinster House, AA; **72/73** National Library Reading Room, AA/S Day; **74** Natural History Museum, AA/M Short; **74/75** Newman's House, AA/S Whitehorne; **76** Royal College of Surgeons, AA/S Day; **76/77** Oscar Wilde's House, AA/M Short; **77** St Ann's Church, AA/S Day; **78** St Stephen's Green, AA/S Day; **78/79** Waterways Visitors Centre, AA/S Day; **80** Traditional Music AA/S Day; **81** Moore Street Market, AA/S Day; **82** Abbey Theatre, AA/S Day; **82/83** Blessington Street Basin, AA/S Day; **84** Casino at Marino, AA/S Whitehorne; **84/85** National Museum Collins Barracks, AA/S Day; **86** Custom House, AA/S Day; **86/87** Custom House, AA/S Whitehorne; **87** Dublin Writer's Museum, AA/M Short; **88/89** Phoenix Park Zoological Gardens, AA/S Whitehorne; **89** Four Courts, AA/S Whitehorne; **90/91** O'Connell Monument, AA/S Day; **92** James Joyce Statue, AA; **94/95** Botanic Gardens Palm House, AA; **96** Old Jameson Distillery, AA/S Day; **96/97** Phoenix Column, AA/S Day; **98/99** St Michan's Church crypt, AA; **99** Smithfield, AA/S Day; **100/101** Malahide Castle, AA; **103t** Avoca, AA/M Short; **103b** Cows at Bective Abbey, AA/C Jones; **104** Claremont Landscape Gardens, AA/D Forss; **104/105** Bray Head, AA/M Short; **106/107** b/g Newgrange, AA/M Short; **107c** Knowth Burial Mound, AA/C Jones; **107b** Bru na Boinne, AA/C Jones; **109** Dalkey, AA/G Munday; **110/111** Magdalene Tower Drogheda, AA/C Jones; **111** Mural Drogheda, AA/P Zoeller; **112** Trafalgar Square Dun Laoghaire, AA/M Short; **112/113** Glendalough, AA/C Jones; **114/115** Hill of Tara, AA/S Day; **115** Howth, AA/M Short; **116/117** John Oxx Stables Kildare, AA/S McBride; **117** Irish National Stud and Japanese Gardens Kildare, AA/S McBride; **118/119** Killiney Bay, AA/S Whitehorne; **119** Monasterboice, AA/M Short; **120/121** Powerscourt Gardens, AA/M Short; **122** Slane Castle, AA/P Zoeller; **123** Trim, AA/C Jones; **124** Poulaphoca Reservoir, AA/M Short; **125** Oysters and Guinness AA/S Day.

Every effort has been made to trace the copyright holders, and we apologise in advance for any unintentional omissions or errors. We would be pleased to apply any corrections in any following edition of this publication.

Maps

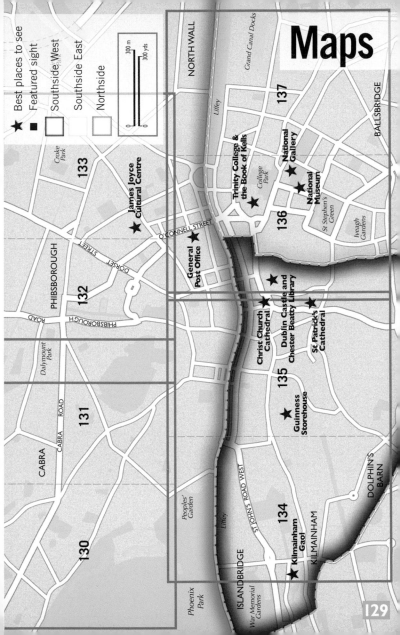

Legend:
- ★ Best places to see
- ■ Featured sight
- ☐ Southside West / Southside East
- ☐ Northside

Scale: 300 m / 300 yds

Grid references and locations:

- 133 — James Joyce Cultural Centre ★ (Croke Park)
- 132 — PHIBSBOROUGH
- 131 — CABRA (Cabra Road)
- 130
- 137 — Grand Canal Docks, BALLSBRIDGE
- National Gallery ★, National Museum ★
- Trinity College & the Book of Kells ★, College Park
- 136 — St Stephen's Green, Iveagh Gardens
- General Post Office ■ (O'Connell Street, Dorset Street)
- Christ Church Cathedral ★, Dublin Castle and Chester Beatty Library ★, St Patrick's Cathedral ★
- 135 — Guinness Storehouse ★
- 134 — Kilmainham Gaol ★, KILMAINHAM, ISLANDBRIDGE, DOLPHIN'S BARN
- Phoenix Park, Peoples' Garden, War Memorial Gardens, Dalymount Park
- NORTH WALL
- Liffey, St John's Road West

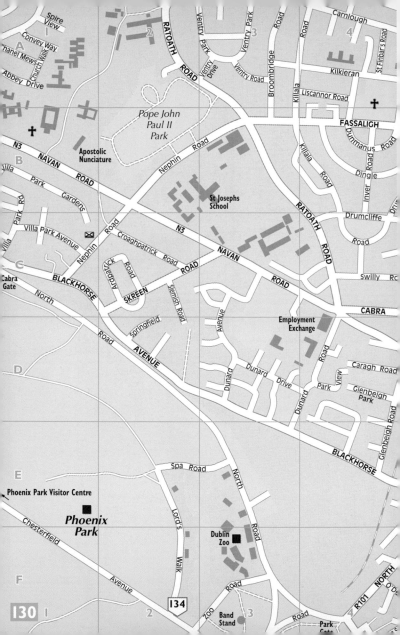

Spire View

Convey Way

hanel Mews

Church Walk

Abbey Drive

RATOATH ROAD

Ventry Park

Ventry Drive

Ventry Park

Ventry Road

Broombridge Road

Road

Carnlough

Kilkieran

St Finbar's Road

Liscannor Road

Pope John Paul II Park

Apostolic Nunciature

Nephin Road

FASSALIGH

Dunmanus Road

Killala Road

Inver Road

Dingle

N3

NAVAN ROAD

B

Villa Park Road

Park Gardens

Villa Park Avenue

Nephin Road

Croaghpatrick Road

St Josephs School

N3

NAVAN ROAD

RATOATH ROAD

Drumcliffe Road

Villa Park

C

Cabra Gate

BLACKHORSE

North Road

Ardpatrick Road

SKREEN

Slemish Road

Springfield

ROAD

NAVAN ROAD

Swilly Rc

CABRA

Employment Exchange

AVENUE

Avenue

Dunard Drive

Dunard Park

Road

View

Caragh Road

Glenbeigh Park

D

Dunard Road

Glenbeigh Road

BLACKHORSE

E

Phoenix Park Visitor Centre

Chesterfield

Spa Road

Lord's Walk

North Road

Phoenix Park

Dublin Zoo

F

Avenue

2

134

Zoo Road

Band Stand

3

Road

R101

NORTH

O'D

Park Gate

130

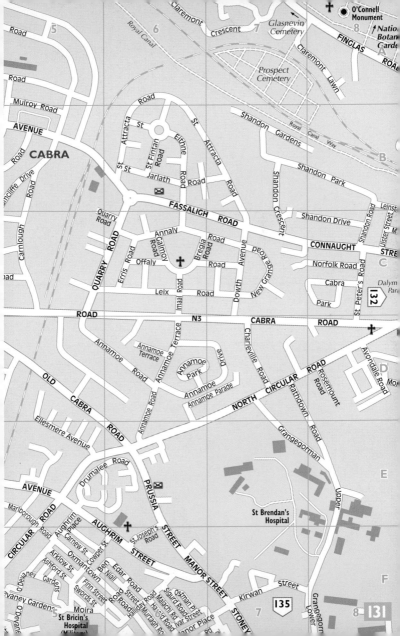

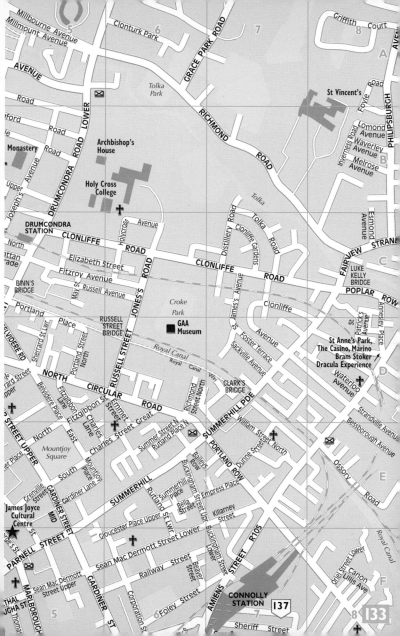

Millbourne Avenue
Millmount Avenue
Clonturk Park
GRACE PARK ROAD
Griffith Court
AVENUE
Road
Tolka Park
RICHMOND
St Vincent's
Road
Road
Road
DRUMCONDRA ROAD LOWER
Monastery
Avenue
Upper's
St Joseph's
Archbishop's House
Holy Cross College
Tolka
Lomond Avenue
Waverley Avenue
Melrose Avenue
Inverness Road
PHILIPSBURGH
Foyle Road

DRUMCONDRA STATION
CLONLIFFE
Holycross Avenue
ROAD
CLONLIFFE ROAD
Distillery Road
Clonliffe Gardens
Tolka Road
Esmond Avenue
FAIRVIEW STRAND
LUKE KELLY BRIDGE
North
Elizabeth street
Fitzroy Avenue
May St
Russell Avenue
JONES'S ROAD
Croke Park
GAA Museum
Clonliffe
Clonliffe Avenue
St Patrick's Avenue
Annesley Place
POPLAR ROW
Mattan rade
BINN'S BRIDGE
Portland Place
Sherrard St Lwr
Portland Street North
RUSSELL STREET BRIDGE
RUSSELL STREET
James's Avenue
Js Foster Terrace
Sackville Avenue
St Anne's Park, The Casino, Marino Bram Stoker Dracula Experience
BELVIDERE RD
Portland
Royal Canal
Royal Canal
Richmond Street North
CLARK'S BRIDGE
Waterloo Avenue
Strandville Avenue
Bessborough Avenue

STREET UPPER
North
Belvidere Place
Fitzgibbon Lane
Fitzgibbon St
Charles Lane
NORTH CIRCULAR ROAD
EMMET STREET
Charles Street Great
SUMMERHILL PDE
Way
William Street North
PORTLAND ROW
Ossory Road

Mountjoy Square
South
Charles Street East
Gardiner Lane
Mountjoy Place
Summer Street N
Rutland Place N
SUMMERHILL
Rutland St Lwr
Bailey's Row
Summerhill Place
Buckingham St Upr
Dunne Street
Strandville Avenue

CARDINER STREET MID
Grenville Street
James Joyce Cultural Centre
PARNELL STREET
Sean Mac Dermott Street Upper
GARDINER STREET
Gloucester Place Upper
Sean Mac Dermott Street Lower
Railway Street
Bella Street
Killarney Street
Empress Place
Buckingham Street Lower
AMIENS STREET
R105
Oriel Street Lower
Canon Lillis Ave
Royal Canal

THAL UGHA ST
MARLBOROUGH
Thomas
Sean Mac Dermott Street Upper
GARDINER ST
Corporation St
Foley Street
Beaver Street
CONNOLLY STATION
137
Sheriff Street

8 **133**

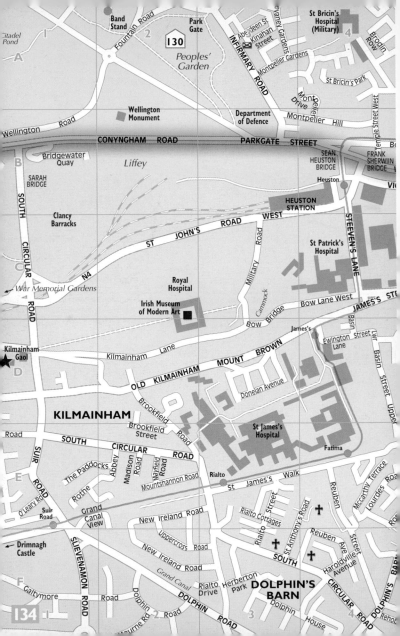

A

Citadel Pond

Band Stand

Fountain Road

Park Gate

Peoples' Garden

130

St Bricin's Hospital (Military) **4**

Brodin Row

Aberdeen St

Kinahan Street

Planey Gardens

Montpelier Gardens

INFIRMARY ROAD

St Bricin's Park

Temple Street West

Wellington Monument

Montpelier Drive

Montpelier Hill

Department of Defence

Wellington Road

CONYNGHAM ROAD

PARKGATE STREET

B

Bridgewater Quay

Liffey

SARAH BRIDGE

SEAN HEUSTON BRIDGE

FRANK SHERWIN BRIDGE

Heuston

VIC

SOUTH

Clancy Barracks

HEUSTON STATION

STEEVEN'S LANE

C

N4

ST JOHN'S ROAD WEST

Military Road

St Patrick's Hospital

CIRCULAR

War Memorial Gardens

Royal Hospital

Camnock

Bow Lane West

JAMES'S STR

ROAD

Irish Museum of Modern Art

Bow Bridge

James's

Basin

Ewington Street Lane

Lwr Basin Street Upper

Kilmainham Lane

James's

D

★ Kilmainham Gaol

OLD KILMAINHAM

MOUNT BROWN

Donelan Avenue

KILMAINHAM

Brookfield Road

St James's Hospital

Brookfield Street

Fatima

Road

SOUTH

CIRCULAR

ROAD

E

The Paddocks

Abbey

Madison Road

Warfield Road

Rialto

St James's Walk

McCarthy Terrace

SUIR

Rothe

Mountshannon Road

Rialto Street

St Anthony's Road

Reuben

Lourdes Avenue

ROAD

Grand Canal View

New Ireland Road

Rialto Cottages

Reuben Ave

Harolville Avenue

O'Leary Road

Suir Road

Uppercross Road

SOUTH

← Drimnagh Castle

SLIEVENAMON ROAD

New Ireland Road

CIRCULAR

DOLPHIN'S

F

Galtymore

Road

Grand Canal

Rialto Drive

Herberton Park

DOLPHIN'S BARN

DOLPHIN ROAD

Dolphin House

Mourne Road

Dolphin Road

134

1

2

3

4

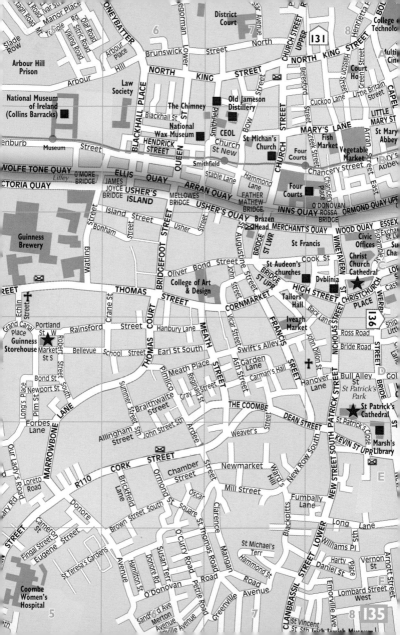

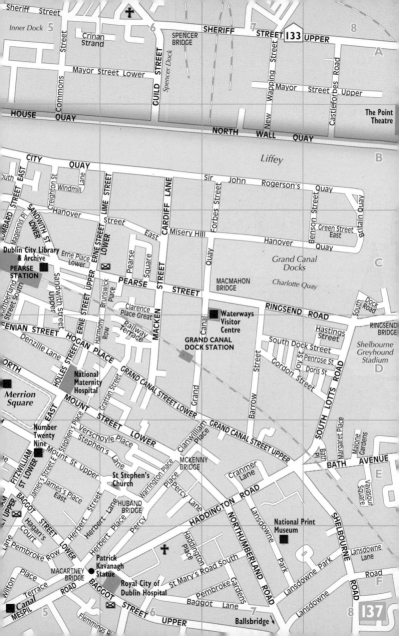

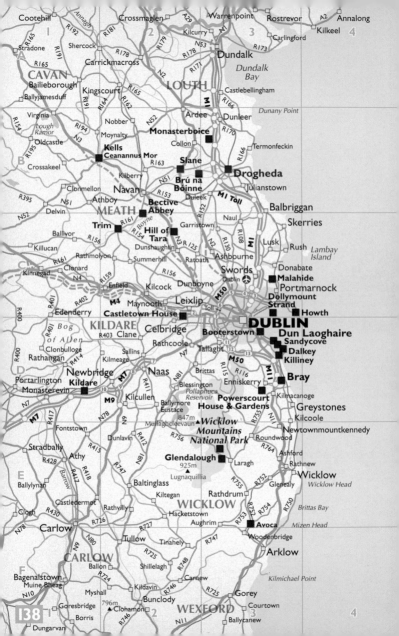

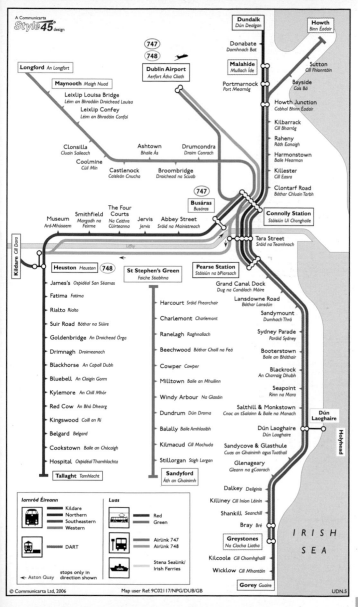

A Communicarta
Style45 design

Howth *Binn Éadair*

Dundalk *Dún Dealgan*

747
748

Dublin Airport *Aerfort Átha Cliath*

Donabate *Domhnach Bat*

Malahide *Mullach Íde*

Portmarnock *Port Mearnóg*

Sutton *Cill Fhionntáin*

Bayside *Cois Bá*

Howth Junction *Cabhal Bhirn Éadair*

Longford *An Longfort*

Maynooth *Maigh Nuad*

Leixlip Louisa Bridge *Léim an Bhradáin Droichead Louisa*
Leixlip Confey *Léim an Bhradáin Confaí*

Kilbarrack *Cill Bharróg*

Raheny *Ráth Eanaigh*

Harmonstown *Baile Hearman*

Killester *Cill Easra*

Clontarf Road *Bóthar Chluain Tarbh*

Clonsilla *Cluain Saileach*
Coolmine *Cúil Mín*
Castleknock *Caisleán Cnucha*

Ashtown *Bhaile Ás*
Broombridge *Droichead na Scuab*

Drumcondra *Droim Conrach*

747
Busáras *Busáras*

Connolly Station *Stáisiún Uí Chonghaile*

Museum *Ard-Mhúsaem*
Smithfield *Margadh na Feirme*
The Four Courts *Na Ceithre Cúirteanna*
Jervis *Jervis*
Abbey Street *Sráid na Mainistreach*

Tara Street *Sráid na Teamhrach*

Liffey

Kildare *Cill Dara*

Heuston *Heuston*   748

St Stephen's Green *Faiche Stiabhna*

Pearse Station *Stáisiún na bPiarsach*

Grand Canal Dock *Dug na Canálach Móire*

James's *Ospidéal San Séamas*

Fatima *Fatima*

Rialto *Rialto*

Suir Road *Bóthar na Siúire*

Goldenbridge *An Droichead Órga*

Drimnagh *Droimeanach*

Blackhorse *An Capall Dubh*

Bluebell *An Cloigín Gorm*

Kylemore *An Chill Mhór*

Red Cow *An Bhó Dhearg*

Kingswood *Coill an Rí*

Belgard *Belgard*

Cookstown *Baile an Chócaigh*

Hospital *Ospidéal Thamhlachta*

Tallaght *Tamhlacht*

Harcourt *Sráid Fhearchair*

Charlemont *Charlemont*

Ranelagh *Raghnallach*

Beechwood *Bóthar Choill na Feá*

Cowper *Cowper*

Milltown *Baile an Mhuilinn*

Windy Arbour *Na Glasáin*

Dundrum *Dún Droma*

Balally *Baile Amhlaoibh*

Kilmacud *Cill Mochuda*

Stillorgan *Stigh Lorgan*

Sandyford *Áth an Ghainimh*

Lansdowne Road *Bóthar Lansdún*

Sandymount *Dumhach Thrá*

Sydney Parade *Pairéid Sydney*

Booterstown *Baile an Bhóthair*

Blackrock *An Charraig Dhubh*

Seapoint *Rinn na Mara*

Salthill & Monkstown *Cnoc an tSalainn & Baile na Manach*

Dún Laoghaire *Dún Laoghaire*

Sandycove & Glasthule *Cuas an Ghainimh agus Tuathail*

Glenageary *Gleann na gCaorach*

Dún Laoghaire

Holyhead

Dalkey *Deilginis*

Killiney *Cill Inion Léinin*

Shankill *Seanchill*

Bray *Bré*

Greystones *Na Clocha Liatha*

Kilcoole *Cill Chomhghaill*

Wicklow *Cill Mhantáin*

Gorey *Guaire*

IRISH SEA

Iarnród Éireann
Kildare
Northern
Southeastern
Western

DART

← Aston Quay   stops only in direction shown

Luas
Red
Green

Airlink 747
Airlink 748

Stena Sealink/
Irish Ferries

© Communicarta Ltd, 2006   Map user Ref: 9C02117/NPG/DUB/GB

UDN.5

139

Notes